Co-Branding

The Science of Alliance

Editors

Tom Blackett

Bob Boad

Interbrand

First published 1999 by
MACMILLAN PRESS LTD
Houndmills, Basingstoke, Hampshire RG21 6XS
and London
Companies and representatives
throughout the world

ISBN 0–333–76089–1

A catalogue record for this book is available from
the British Library.

This book is printed on paper suitable for recycling and
made from fully managed and sustained forest sources.

10   9   8   7   6   5   4   3   2   1
08 07 06 05 04 03 02 01 00 99

Designed and formatted by
The Ascenders Partnership, Basingstoke
Illustrations by Ascenders

Printed in Great Britain by
Creative Print & Design (Wales),
Ebbw Vale

Contents

3 **The Risks and Pitfalls of Co-Branding**   **38**
Bob Boad

4 **Co-Branding – a Retailer's Opportunity**   **47**
Mark Linnell

The Future of Co-Branding   **113**

8 Tom Blackett, Bob Boad, Paul Cowper and
Shailendra Kumar

List of Tables and Figures

List of Illustrations

Preface

Leslie de Chernatony
Beneficial Bank Professor of Brand Marketing

CO-BRANDING, if used properly, can be a very effective strategy that benefits both the participating organizations and customers. Much has been written about strategic alliances and joint ventures, but little has been written about co-branding. It is therefore most welcoming to see this book which advances our understanding of this important topic.

Branding is about adding value and co-branding is testimony to this, particularly as the aim is to ensure that the resultant entity has a value greater than the value of the component parts. It involves a visionary perspective about how to make the world a better place, and creativity to conceive the innovative cluster of benefits. It necessitates a strategic orientation that then considers how the two players can realign their value chains to deliver the promised value and jointly capitalize on the resultant rewards. As this book so lucidly shows, adopting a tactical, short-term perspective on co-branding does not take advantage of the true potential from strategically leveraging the competitive advantage from a new bundle of benefits.

From an organizational perspective, co-branding represents an opportunity for a win-win scenario. As we move away from the era of transaction brand marketing to relationship brand marketing, co-branding is doubtless going to become an even more important strategy for co-producing enhanced value. This book not only provides well argued insights about getting the most from co-branding, but also covers some very useful application issues.

Different managers have different interpretations of co-branding and a strength of this book is that it provides a clear definition of co-branding. What we are then able to appreciate are the different levels of co-branding and through the typology presented in this book, the indigestion caused by diverse interpretations about co-branding is calmed and a clearer route forward presented.

As sources of added value become more difficult to identify, co-branding presents an opportunity for leapfrogging competition to win the hearts and minds of consumers. Some consumers purchase brands in a 'risk reducing mode' where they feel uncertain about how the brand will perform. Co-branding therefore presents an opportunity for greater consumer reassurance and could switch a cautionary purchasing perspective to one of pride enhancement.

There is much in this book that is invaluable to managers seeking to capitalize on co-branding. Well-considered frameworks rapidly enable ideas to form about how to embark on a co-branding strategy and much practical advice is presented. A particularly helpful framework is presented at the end of the book which helps managers identify potential co-branding partners. This timely book has much to offer.

Professor Leslie de Chernatony
Beneficial Bank Professor of Brand Marketing

Acknowledgements

Tom Blackett

I would first like to acknowledge the skill and support throughout this project of my co-editor Bob Boad. The idea to write this book came from Bob and for both of us it has been a true voyage of discovery. Bob is a talented writer who over the years has made many contributions to the diary columns of the country's leading broadshcets. His style illuminates the chapters he has written and he tackles this subject from a hase of firm experience.

Next I must acknowledge the contributions made by the other chapter authors. The 'Interbrand brigade' – Nick Russell, Paul Cowper, Jan Lindemann, Shailendra Kumar and Marc Smit – rose to the challenge I gave them and wrote fluently and informatively on their allotted subjects. Mark Linnell on the other hand, is a new friend – and an informed and experienced one too. Mark has 'been there, done that, etc.' and speaks as one well versed in the ways of co-branding. His contribution is greatly valued.

Thanks must also go to Emma Baptist for managing the project, Catherine Jackson for her research and preparation, Susannah Hart for her observations and recommendations and Jez Fraser for his designs. Valerie Edelson of IBM was very kind and helpful. Many other people have been involved in the preparation of this book and many companies have given us insight into their worlds. We are most grateful to them.

Bob Boad

I too am enormously grateful to the many kind people who have assisted and encouraged me in this venture.

I now understand why authors always mention spouses or partners in the Preface to their books and so I would like to particularly acknowledge the sacrifices and contributions that my wife Roma has made during the year it took for this selfish venture to move from being a vague idea, through being a steadily growing pile of paper and sample packs that occupied the dining table at weekends, before eventually evolving into the completed manuscript. Trips to the shops will not be the same without my habitual scouring of the shelves for the latest example of co-branding!

Although it was a purely personal project, the approval in principle of my employees, BP Amoco p.l.c., was welcomed and I hope that some of my colleagues may find the finished volume of interest. The suggestions and general encouragement provided by many friends in the company, particularly Robin Hadfield and others in the Group Trade Marks team, Thomas Golsong of the Global Brand team, Paul Giblett of BP Middle East, Daya Chetty of TATA BP Lubricants Ltd, David Brooks of BP Oil UK, Fiona MacLeod of BP Oil New Zealand and Michael Gasson and Katy Green in the BP Archive have all been greatly appreciated.

I am also very grateful for the advice and contributions made by trademark attorneys and practitioners in many parts of the globe: Todd Bontemps of Cooley Godward (US), Christine Lowe of Davies Collinson Cave (Australia), David Castle of Castles (UK), Ian Wood of Rowe & Maw (UK), Ben Ely of Rouse & Co International (UK), Evan Kent of Russ, August & Kabat (US) and Mike Mlotkowski of Mobil Oil Corporation (US).

Thank you to all of the brand owners who have co-operated with me, especially André Cointreau and Clare Crago of Le Cordon Bleu, Mike Heller of Cisco Systems, Courtney Petersen and Peter Gretton of Telstra, Graham Minton of WWF, Richard Richardson of Harry Ramsden's, Liz Topham of Young's.

Finally, I would like to thank my co-author Tom Blackett for enthusiastically embracing this idea and 'making it happen'. It seemed entirely appropriate to write a book on this topic with a co-author and in 'practising what I preach' in this book I thought very carefully about with whom I should 'co-brand' and I could not have made a better choice than Tom. Aided by his colleagues at Interbrand – especially Catherine Jackson, Emma Baptist, Nick Russell, Paul Cowper, Jan Lindemann, Susannah Hart and Marc Smit – and his friend Mark Linnell, Tom has researched this fascinating topic very thoroughly and developed the concept far beyond anything that I had originally envisaged or could have produced alone.

Tom and Bob

We would both like to acknowledge the enthusiastic support we have had from Stephen Rutt and Victoria Capstick at the publisher.

Finally we would like to express our gratitude to Professor Leslie de Chernatony, Beneficial Bank Professor of Brand Marketing at The Open University for his complimentary comments on the manuscript and for kindly writing a Preface for inclusion herein.

List of Contributors

Tom Blackett

Tom is deputy chairman of Interbrand Group plc. He started his career in market research, joining Attwood Statistics in 1969. Three years later he moved to Research Bureau Limited, then Unilever's in-house market research agency, where he became intensively involved in new product research and simulated market testing. In 1978 he moved to Inbucon Management Consultants (now part of the PE Group) where he specialized in new product development across a wide range of consumer, business-to-business and industrial markets. Clients included Distillers Company Limited, Heinz, Beecham, Reckitt and Colman and Quaker.

Tom joined Interbrand in 1983 and since then has seen the company grow from a specialist brand naming 'boutique' to a broad-based consultancy with skills in brand and corporate identity, brand strategy, brand valuation, new product development and trademark law.

Tom has led projects for a large number of international clients including Heineken, Unilever, Mobil, British Telecom and ICI. He has written and spoken widely on the subject of brands and his book *Trademarks* was published by Macmillan in 1998.

Bob Boad

Bob is a UK Registered Trade Mark Attorney and European Trade Mark Attorney. For the last 15 years he has been employed as Senior Trade Marks Adviser to BP Amoco p.l.c., one of the world's largest oil and petrochemical companies. Prior to that he held a similar position at Wellcome, the pharmaceutical company which has now merged with Glaxo. He is based in London but travels extensively in connection with his employment. Currently he has particular responsibility for BP Amoco's retail trademarks, including the global project to protect their distinctive green service-station livery.

Bob started his career in marketing, having been sponsored by Wellcome on a Business Studies degree but in his mid-twenties he switched to work and study in the trade marks field. However, he has retained a keen interest in marketing matters, particularly those involving brands.

Bob has made many presentations on brand and trademark issues, including a recent paper on the protection of colour as a trademark at the Fordham University School of Law, Intellectual Property Conference in New York, a presentation to the International Anti-Counterfeiting Coalition and various lectures and seminars for student members of the UK Institute of Trade Mark Attorneys. His main hobby is writing and this includes regular contributions of brand-related items to several UK newspapers.

Paul Cowper

Paul is a consultant in the Brand Development department. Paul previously spent three years working in Design dealing with projects for Elida Fabergé, Birds Eye Walls, Cogesal, McVities, Grand Met, Pernod Ricard and Bayer.

Paul is a graduate of Sheffield Hallam University with a degree in History of Art, Design and Film. Since joining Interbrand in October 1997 Paul has worked on innovation projects for Holsten, Taisho and American Express.

Jan Lindemann

Jan is a Director of Interbrand's global brand valuation practice. He has worked on numerous brand valuation assignments including multinational companies such as Texas Instruments and ICI. Prior to joining Interbrand, Jan worked as Mergers & Acquisitions advisor for The Chase Manhattan Bank. His clients included multinational companies such as Electrolux, United Technologies, Mannesmann and Gulf Air.

Jan holds a masters degree in history, philosophy and political science from the Free University of Berlin, Germany and a masters degree in international economics and international politics from The School of Advanced International Studies of The John Hopkins University, Washington DC, USA.

Shailendra Kumar

Shailendra graduated from University College London where he read Economics and an intercollegiate programme in International Relations at the London School of Economics. He was at PricewaterhouseCoopers in London for seven years where he qualified as a Chartered Accountant. After qualification he helped set up the PW global shareholder value practice managing international consulting and valuation assignments for clients including Sony (Japan), British Airways Plc and Rank Organisation Plc.

Shailendra joined the Brand Valuation team at Interbrand in November 1997 and since then has worked in major brand valuation and strategey assignments in the utilities industry in the US, Canada and South Africa. In addition, he has conducted brand valuations in the petroleum industry in the US, and the Hi-Tech sector in the Far East. Shailendra has also written and published articles on the subject of brands, marketing and finance.

Mark Linnell

Mark has considerable experience of the convenience store industry and also of running his own sales and marketing company. He was a director of Neighbourhood Stores plc, the 7-Eleven UK licensee, where he was responsible for establishing strategic alliances with the oil industry. Mark has also been the sales director of McLane UK Limited, a specialist distribution company. McLane Company in the United States is the world's largest convenience store distributor and subsidiary of Wal-Mart Inc., the world's largest retailer.

Mark's company, Market Enterprises (UK) Limited specializes in establishing strategic alliances for retailers and for companies wishing to work with retailers.

Nick Russell

Nick has responsibility for Interbrand's Brand Operations practice in London. He previously worked with PricewaterhouseCoopers, where he designed and led long term organizational change and process re-engineering programmes for, among others, Dow Chemical, Tetra Pak, Baxter Healthcare, Bose Corporation, Nuclear Electric, British Nuclear Fuels and British Rail. In all these cases, the objective achieved was an increase in customer orientation and commercial awareness among the workforce.

Before entering consultancy, Nick worked in telecoms and television. He was consumer marketing manager for BT's interactive videotex service (Prestel), a forerunner to the Internet. He was also marketing manager for Premiere, a cable TV movie channel, for which he managed the initial positioning of the brand.

Nick has a psychology degree from Durham University and an MBA from London Business School.

Marc Smit

After graduating from ICHEC in Brussels with a Business Administration degree, Marc worked in the European headquarters of DuPont Pharma in Frankfurt, as well as at CLT-UFA (audio-visual arm of Bertelsmann AG), respectively, dealing with activity-based accounting and acquisition/valuation. Thereafter he decided to enrol in the MBA programme at Rotterdam School of Management. He started working at Interbrand as a consultant in 1998.

Introduction

IT WAS HG Wells who observed that brands 'let the manufacturer reach over the shoulder of the retailer straight to the consumer' but even that great visionary did not foresee the explosion of interest that we are experiencing today in bringing independent brands together upon a single product or service. Had his thoughts turned to the subject of co-branding he might have gone on to say that it enabled manufacturers – and retailers too – to target more accurately the exact desires of consumers. Markets are becoming increasingly sophisticated and demand offers that are more finely tuned; co-branding is a tool which is ideal for satisfying those aspirations

Many companies nowadays are experimenting with co-branding, recognizing that the strong mutuality of interest which informs such ventures, if properly handled, can provide a 'win-win'. If it is not properly handled, however, then one or both partners will suffer and, most importantly, the brands concerned may become tarnished. As 'branding people', it struck us as incongruous that in the vast majority of business alliances that take place the brands concerned are frequently the last assets to be considered – if they are considered at all. (In BP's case this is certainly not the case as the company jealously guards its trademarks and is particularly careful when it comes to 'partnering' these with those of other companies). What also struck us was how little has been written about co-branding, hence this book.

'Co-branding' is a term that is nowadays bandied about for a very wide range of marketing activities involving the use of two (and occasionally more) brand names. These can appear in juxtaposition on credit and charge cards, the side of cola cans, packaging for potato crisps, personal computers, motor cars – the list is endless. But to what extent is co-branding, which to us purists represents the mutual enhancement of two brands through close association on a product or service, just that – or lazy shorthand for a joint venture? This is something that has absorbed us in this book – not through some narrow obsession with the subject, but because we believe co-branding to be a legitimate offspring of branding. And branding is now widely acknowledged as a business discipline of the highest importance in the creation of competitive advantage and, ultimately, shareholder value.

In our simple way we believe that if companies decide to pool their resources in the pursuit of a business opportunity and describe this as co-branding, then they should be aware of what this means. The reality may be that the deal is no more than just a joint venture, where credit card operator A agrees to partner bank B to launch a new gold card. The presence of both parties' names on the card could lead us to conclude that this is co-branding. But if the driving purpose for the partners is to boost capacity utilization on the one hand, and attract and retain customers on the other, then the term 'co-branding' must be seen in perspective. Here it can only be described as a mechanism rather than a commercial objective – the means to an end rather than the end in itself.

Whether or not companies planning joint ventures take their brands into consideration, one thing is sure: their use in tandem will almost certainly affect the way customers perceive them. If the partners are well matched, the strategy sound and the resulting product or service attractive and desirable, then the chances are that the brands will both benefit. (The strong synergies that have arisen between Intel and the PC manufacturers spring to mind). But if the match is ill-considered and opportunistic, then the chances are considerably less that such a result will occur. (Here less attractive images of the offspring of lustful alley cats arise).

Any partnership arrangement in business carries a level of risk – and where brands are also to be involved the risk increases. Managers will of course take steps to ensure that the risks involved in a partnership are minimized – but how often will the 'due diligence' take into account the brands? It seems to us that if the key issues regarding the protection and enhancement of brand values in business alliances can be identified, then this will go a long way towards helping companies who are interested in exploring this strategy for developing their businesses.

In this book, therefore, we look at those companies who in the pursuit of business development have sometimes chosen the 'partnership route'. We have been particularly interested to see how co-branding practice has grown out of joint venture – or alliance – management practice, as the partners concerned have come to learn how their brands act as receptacles for the customer goodwill arising from the successful union. From this some useful lessons can be learned.

We look too at the legal and financial issues to be considered in entering and managing co-branding relationships. These are frequently complex and, because of that, poorly understood areas. Perhaps this is because the training given to company brand managers still fails to equip them for the full requirements of their task. This is why in many organizations, ultimate responsibility for the brand increasingly is vested in the CEO and his colleagues. Co-branding is a further complication for them to get to grips with.

As economists, the business schools, and any pundit worth his salt continue to remind us: escalating consumer demand over the next few years will drive up world trade to unprecedented levels; 'producer countries' will proliferate; and the world may begin to divide between those countries that make things and those countries that own the 'intellectual property' concerned. Whatever, it seems increasingly unlikely that many companies, other than the biggest, will possess the resources to take advantage of such extraordinary opportunities for growth. The increasing trend we have seen over the last few years towards business alliances and joint ventures therefore seems certain to continue – and with it the rise of co-branding.

It would be misleading to claim that this book enshrines 'best practice' for the use of co-branding. Co-branding is still in its infancy and successful examples of the genre are relatively rare. It would be fairer to say that we have tried to draw attention to the need to do it properly, to raise awareness that co-branding is not just a 'logo scattering' exercise, and that it must be considered as an extremely important strategy the consequences of which can profoundly affect the future of the business.

So we hope that what first suggested itself to us as an interesting topic for research will prove to be of value to all businesses seeking to develop through partnership. Sufficient has probably been written about the strategic and commercial niceties of seeking and nurturing profitable business partnerships, and it is not our intention here to go over such well-worn ground. Rather we concentrate on the brand, recognizing that of all the assets of a business it is probably the brand that offers, potentially, the greatest long-term security for its owner.

Tom Blackett
Bob Boad

1 What is Co-Branding?

Tom Blackett and Nick Russell

*People of the same trade seldom meet together, even for merriment
and diversion, but the conversation ends in a conspiracy against the
public, or in some contrivance to raise prices.*   **Adam Smith**

OVER THE last twenty years we have witnessed extraordinary growth in
world trade. Much of this has been driven by developments in central and
eastern Europe, Asia and the Latin American countries, where rapidly
increasing prosperity has created huge markets for consumer goods and
services which Western companies have been quick to exploit. In the more
mature markets too there has been steady growth accompanied by
technological developments, which a few years ago would have been quite
inconceivable. These factors, underpinned by a period of unprecedented
geopolitical stability, have helped to create a climate of commercial opportunity
that is unmatched in the history of the world.

For many companies in a hurry, the formation of alliances and joint ventures
with like-minded partners provides the way ahead, and co-branding is a
common manifestation of such enterprises. But the term 'co-branding' is
relatively new to the business vocabulary and is used to encompass a wide
range of marketing activity involving the use of two (and sometimes more)
brands. Thus co-branding could be considered to include sponsorship, where
Marlboro lends its name to Ferrari or accountants Ernst and Young support the
Monet exhibition; retail promotion, where BP and Disney get together; retailing
itself, where BP forecourts 'host' Safeway mini-stores; manufacturing collaborations – the Mercedes-Swatch car; or film-making, where Miramax
produces and Buena Vista distributes. The list of possibilities is endless.

But what precisely is co-branding? Why has it grown in popularity amongst
– and between – such a diverse range of businesses? And what does it signify
as far as the future of branding and marketing is concerned? To answer these
questions we should first examine more closely the motive for brand
ownership.

The Importance of Brands

The word brand comes down to us from the old Norse word 'brandr' meaning to burn. By branding their livestock early humankind could mark their owner-ship and distinguish their cattle from those of their neighbours. Thus the primary role of the brand was established: to identify ownership or origin.

With the development of trade, the makers of goods were quick to realize the benefit that their brand could confer. Some of the earliest manufactured goods in 'mass' production were clay pots, the remains of which can be found in great abundance in the countries of the Mediterranean. There is considerable evidence of the use of brands; in their earliest form these were potters' mark, but these gradually became more sophisticated through the use of names or devices, in the form of a cross or star. In Ancient Rome, principles of commercial law developed which acknowledged the origin and title of potters' marks but this did not deter manufacturers of inferior pots from imitating the marks of well-known manufacturers in order to dupe the public. There are even examples in the British Museum of imitation Roman pottery bearing imitation Roman marks; these were probably made in Belgium in the first century AD and designed to fool the illiterate Britons! Thus as trade followed the flag – or eagle – so the insidious practice of unlawful imitation lurked at its heels, a practice which remains commonplace despite the strictures of our modern, highly developed legal systems.

Since the earliest times, therefore, the value of a strong brand has been recognized: by customers who would reward the supplier of good quality produce or merchandise with their custom and loyalty; by the suppliers themselves who knew that their brands symbolized their 'bona fides'; by imitators seeking to obtain an unfair commercial advantage; and by the law.

Brands nowadays are no different. But such is the strategic importance to their owners that increasingly they are regarded as assets in their own right, and subject to investment and evaluation in the same way as other business assets. And just as other business assets can be bought and sold, brands have featured centre stage in some of the biggest public transactions in the late twentieth century. For example, Kohlberg Kravis Roberts, the New York investment house, paid $31billion for RJR Nabisco in 1989. RJR Nabisco was the owner of such famous brands as Winston cigarettes, Oreos cookies and Nabisco crackers. Kohlberg Kravis Roberts interest was not in the tangible assets of this business – the manufacturing plant, the equipment and investments etc. – but in the potential value of these great brands. Similarly, Nestle paid £5 billion for Rowntree in 1988, a price that was five times the disclosed net assets, and twice the previous market capitalization of the company. The reason for the high premium? – ownership of such famous brands as Aero, Smarties and Kit-Kat, brands which Rowntree by itself could not afford adequately to exploit. Many companies now recognize the value of their brands in their financial accounts, and in their recent professional standards paper FRS10, the UK Accounting Standards Board has defined practice for the treatment of brands and other forms of 'intangible' asset on acquisition.

The motive for brand ownership is therefore clear: strong brands, because of their ability to command highly reliable income streams, offer economic benefits that add materially to the value of the organization. This has now been proved beyond reasonable doubt, as this recent comparison by Interbrand of the share price performance of 'branded' organizations with the average of the FTSE 'Top 350' in Figure 1.1 shows. It has also been confirmed in exhaustive research by consultancies like PIMS (Profit Impact of Marketing Strategy), who in a recent report 'Evidence on the contribution of branded consumer businesses to economic growth' concluded:

> For branded consumer businesses, which need to communicate with large numbers of end user purchasers, the rewards of strong market position combined with clear customer preference can be large. Higher share consumer businesses find it much easier to turn a quality advantage into profitable returns than those with weaker share. For ...'unbranded' consumer businesses, which includes suppliers of store brands ... the rewards to both scale and quality are smaller and less predictable.

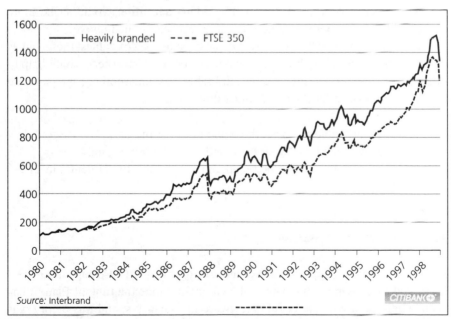

Figure 1.1 Share price performance of 'branded' organizations with the average of the FTSE 'Top 350'

'Rare and Precious Assets'

Thus an increasing proportion of modern businesses treat their brands as valuable assets, to be nurtured and sustained through careful management and development. The best brands have unique distinguishing characteristics, and it is the pursuit of these attributes that involves the activities of an army of brand managers, advertising agencies, graphic designers and branding consultancies, supported by lawyers and accountants. Each in their own way seeks an explanation of how their brand works; if this can be done then, rationally, it must be possible to create ways in which the brand can be managed so as to maximize profitability and minimize risk. Unlike Euclidean geometry, however, the art of brand management carries no such certainties, as we shall explain.

Of all the diverse parties whose fortunes are linked to brands it is the lawyers – perhaps predictably – who have come closest to codifying brands. A lawyer will define a brand as a trademark, a piece of distinct intellectual property. And the lawyer will define a trademark as 'Any sign capable of being represented graphically which is capable of distinguishing the goods or services of one undertaking from those of another undertaking' because this is the wording of the UK Trade Marks Act 1994. In practice, of course, a brand is much more. Perhaps a handier definition would be 'A mixture of tangible and intangible values symbolized in a trademark which, if properly managed, creates value and ensures influence on a market over time'. This definition would strike more chords with those other disparate interest groups mentioned above.

A brand, therefore, is the polyvisual expression of a set of values; these values are built on impressions about the product or service concerned, which help to differentiate the product or service in a desirable way, and motivate the purchase decision. Values can be classified under three headings:

1. 'Functional' values – 'what the brand does for me';
2. 'Expressive' values – 'what the brand says about me'; and
3. 'Central' values – 'what the brand and I share at a fundamental level'.

How Brands Appeal

A brand's values can appeal in one or more of four ways. These appeals are best illustrated by looking at the nature of awareness. Since the time of Plato it has been widely believed that people are aware in four ways, and this theory was used by Jung in his teaching on human psychology. He gave the four functions of the mind specific names:

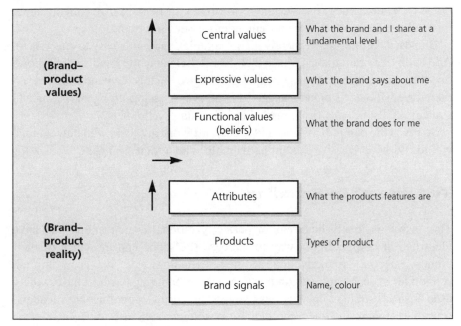

Figure 1.2 Brand value ladder
Source: Interbrand

1. Thinking, which deals with logic and rationale;
2. Sensation, which is the direct perception of phenomena;
3. Feeling, which is concerned with emotions; and
4. Intuition, which is the ability to sense the intangible in a situation.

We are aware in all these four ways; we are open to four kinds of appeal and this means that brands can appeal in a number of ways. For years companies like Procter & Gamble have built brands based on strong rational and sensational appeals: Crest helps prevent cavities, Tide washes whiter; Ivory Soap has a highly distinctive fragrance, Pringles potato crisps have unique texture and flavour. Finding and exploiting such functional values, however, is increasingly difficult, so brands that also possess strong emotional and intuitive appeals can become powerful assets.

Emotion-led brands strike a chord that can influence at the most fundamental level. This fact has not escaped many of the world's leading insurance companies who have for years played on cherished values – family, children, future financial security. Emotion-led brands are introverted, while intuitive brands are extroverted. Marlboro advertising conveys a point about intuitive-led brands – the cowboy, the West, the carefully cultivated mythology of nearly one hundred years of Hollywood hokum. Consumers identify with intuitive brands because they enable them to make a personal statement about themselves; these appeals are a tremendous asset for a brand.

Brands, therefore, are frequently highly complex and rarely easy to understand. Add to this the often-quoted truism that 'brands belong in the mind' and it follows that their stewardship can pose unique challenges. Such is the nature of the task, therefore, that today's brand manager, as well as possessing strong marketing and strategic skills, needs a firm grasp of behavioural psychology.

So given the complexity, cost and sheer hard work involved who but a lunatic would risk his precious brand in partnership with a total stranger?

The Rise of Co-Branding

The answer is, many hundreds of perfectly rational organizations that have identified in co-branding a way to increase the scope and influence of their brands, enter new markets, embrace new technologies, reduce costs through economies of scale, and refresh their image. Co-branding has become a widely used business strategy in industries like food and drinks, retailing, air travel and financial services. In 1994, according to consultants McKinsey & Company, the number of corporate alliances worldwide – including co-branding ventures – was growing at 40 per cent each year, involving millions of dollars in assets. Not only were there more partnerships, but these were getting bigger and becoming more central to marketers' overall strategies. In some cases the practice had redefined entire categories; in credit cards, for example, McKinsey estimated that co-branding accounted for about one-third of the $473 billion in charge card volume, up 20 per cent over the previous two years. It could be argued, of course, that branding in the financial services industry is still in its infancy and that brand owners have little to lose through an incautious alliance; but the leading partners in co-branding deals are such financial services veterans as MasterCard, Visa, American Express and Diners. These, by any criteria, are distinguished brands and capable of keeping company with the very best.

Co-Branding – the Interbrand Definition

In order to provide helpful advice to those seeking to make a success of a co-branding venture, we need to have a clear understanding of what is and what is not a co-branding arrangement, what each party typically brings to the venture and what benefits each is likely to gain from their involvement.

It should not need saying that the basis for any co-operative arrangement is the expectation of synergies which create value for both participants, over and above the value they would expect to generate on their own. That principle, however, does not help us to discriminate between co-branding, promotions, alliances and joint ventures; it should apply to them all.

At Interbrand, our work has led us to the conclusion that two main criteria determine both the category of co-operation to which a particular venture belongs and the nature of the practical arrangements that are likely to be required. They are first, the expected duration of the co-operative relationship and, second, the nature and amount of potential value that can be created through sharing or co-operation.

Figure 1.3 shows these two criteria positioned as the axes of a typical consultant's matrix. Linking the two criteria in this way and positioning real-life examples on the matrix clarifies how the various types of co-operation differ and shows the area of the co-operation continuum that is generally described as co-branding.

We have reached a definition of co-branding for this book by examining real instances discussed in the literature or described as such by their participants, though this causes it to be bounded by what it is not rather than describing exhaustively what it is. Co-branding is a form of co-operation between two or more brands with significant customer recognition, in which all the participants' brand names are retained. It is usually of medium-to long-term duration and its net value creation potential is too

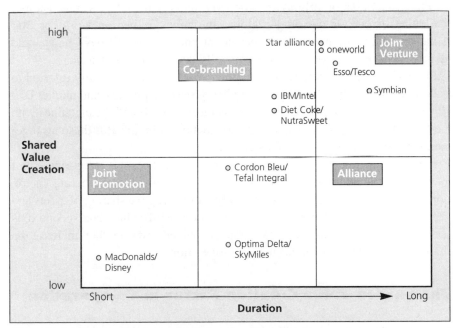

Figure 1.3 Co-branding distinguished from other forms of co-operative venture
Source: Interbrand

small to justify setting up a new brand and/or legal joint venture.

Logic and experience confirm that the stronger the brands are that form the co-brand, the more likely it is that their identities will be preserved, whatever the extent of co-operation. If the participants were to destroy significant value by abandoning very powerful brands and investing resources in another name instead, the net value creation potential would be severely reduced.

The Duration Factor in Different Types of Co-operation

Co-operative relationships can vary in duration from three months to ten years, depending on the life-cycle of the products and/or the characteristics of the markets involved. Thus, McDonald's and Disney might co-operate on merchandising and promotion for the McDonald's product range using the themes and characters from the latest Disney movie such as The Lion King or Pocahontas. This will typically last for three to four months and can best be defined as a co-promotion.

At the other extreme, Mercedes-Benz and Swatch are co-operating on the development, manufacture and launch of a new urban vehicle, a process likely to take a minimum of five years. This is best described as a joint venture. Similarly, a number of airlines are co-operating on routes, flights and customer marketing in one of two major global initiatives, either oneworld or Star Alliance. These initiatives have no evident endpoint at all, have new brand identities created for them, and are generally described as alliances.

In between these extremes lie a number of arrangements usually referred to as co-branding, such as Coca-Cola with NutraSweet to produce and market Diet Coke or Intel with a variety of PC manufacturers to co-brand the machines with the 'Intel Inside' logo alongside the manufacturer's brand. But these arrangements do not have fixed endpoints either.

It appears that envisioned duration strongly influences the categorization of many instances of co-operation, but is not the only discriminating factor. Longer-term co-operations generally imply more extensive sharing of assets and expertise, with the potential to generate more shared value. The second axis seeks to depict what assets and expertise are shared and how they increase the shared value creation potential in the co-operation.

The Shared Value Creation Factor in Co-operation

Examining the nature of a variety of successful and unsuccessful co-operations leads us to the conclusion that there is a hierarchy of types of shared value creation opportunity and they seem to be linked to the nature of the co-operation and the term used to describe it. Figure 1.4 below illustrates this hierarchy and is followed by a detailed discussion of each of the four types.

Reach–Awareness Co-Branding

The lowest level of shared involvement and hence value creation occurs in situations where co-operation enables the parties rapidly to increase awareness of their brand through exposure to their partner's customer base. Many direct marketing-based co-operations are justified on this basis and co-branding relationships between credit card suppliers and other parties illustrate the principle well.

American Express, for instance, launched a co-branded version of its new Optima credit card in concert with Delta Airlines SkyMiles programme and invited SkyMiles members to sign up. For the members, the benefit was that they gained SkyMiles (redeemable for free flights) in return for the dollars they spent using the card. American Express gained users and transactions for its Optima card and Delta enriched the benefits package it could offer to its SkyMiles members, increasing their loyalty to that programme and hence their likelihood of using Delta flights.

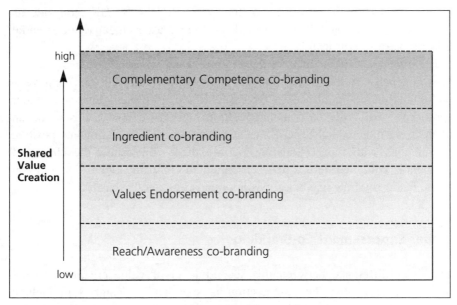

Figure 1.4 Hierarchy of types of value creation sharing in co-operative
relationships

Source: Interbrand

In this relationship, the two companies co-operated on marketing and promotional activities and maintain ongoing co-operation in order for Delta to credit their SkyMiles members with miles, according to their level of spend. However, there are few intrinsic links between the Optima and Delta SkyMiles brands and no need for close complementarity in brand values. Equally, Optima could, and did, forge similar arrangements with other membership–loyalty schemes, demonstrating that co-branding partnerships are not always unique.

Operationally, a relatively low level of joint investment and action were required to make the co-brand work; SkyMiles could handle the mailings on its own and Optima could register the transactions through its own infrastructure. Recording the miles earned by each customer is straightforward and can be communicated to SkyMiles in a periodic bulk data transfer.

Many other consumer marketing companies have set up similar co-branding relationships with a bank that is tied to one or other of the main credit card processing companies (Visa, MasterCard, Diners Club) or with the processing company directly. While the benefits to the processing company remain constant (additional users generating transaction volume), there is some variation in the benefit to the consumer marketing company. For example, while SkyMiles was primarily interested to broaden the range of benefits for existing members, when General Motors and Visa launched a co-branded credit card in the UK, it enabled GM to build awareness of the GM brand in the UK alongside its familiar Vauxhall brand. It also enabled GM to increase its database of potential UK purchasers significantly.

In summary, at this lowest level of joint value creation, each of the co-branding partners has benefits and revenue opportunities it can achieve – including but not confined to increased brand awareness among a wider audience – from the co-branding relationship. There also needs to be an identifiable incremental benefit for the consumers that will stimulate positive associations with the co-branding. Within these constraints, the choice of partners is wide and tie-ups between unrelated companies with few common brand features (strategy, values, positioning) are perfectly feasible.

Values Endorsement Co-Branding

The chief difference between this second level of value creation and the previous one is that the co-operation is specifically designed to include endorsement of one or other's brand values and positioning or both. In fact, it is often a principal reason for the tie-up. Credit cards again provide a good way of illustrating the concept. In recent years many charities have launched co-branded 'affinity' credit cards with a bank or transaction processing company, in fact so many that the concept has been somewhat devalued but the principle remains intact.

The original underlying concept is that the bank or transaction processor gives a small proportion of its transaction revenue back to the charity as 'commission' for the cardholders it introduced. So the charity benefits from extra revenue, the bank–processor receives extra transaction volume and the customer gets a warm glow from feeling that he/she has given more to his/her favourite cause – without it costing a penny! In addition, the bank–processor gains kudos and positive associations for its brand because it is 'sacrificing' some of its revenue to the good cause that the customer values.

This is a good deal for the bank–processor, as it can be argued that all they are contributing is the marketing budget they would have had to use to acquire new subscribers anyway, but insofar as they overspend that budget they are investing to develop positive values for their brand.

There are considerable similarities between this arrangement and traditional corporate sponsorships, in which a company donates to a worthy public cause in return for publicity for its brand. The brand comes to be associated in the public mind with the worthy cause and with positive 'good citizen' brand values. Classic examples of this are Texaco's long-running sponsorship of the Metropolitan Opera in New York and Royal Insurance's sponsorship of the Royal Shakespeare Company in the UK.

So the essence of value endorsement co-branding is that the two participant companies co-operate because they have, or want to achieve, alignment of their brand values in the customer's mind. This substantially decreases the pool of potential partners for any projected co-branding deal and increases the value creation potential, compared to the brand awareness objective seen in first-level co-branding.

Le Cordon Bleu's co-branding deal with Tefal offers a more conventional example of value endorsement co-branding. Le Cordon Bleu is a French culinary academy whose brand has become synonymous with the highest standards of cooking. Tefal, a leading French cookware manufacturer, was launching its new 'Integral' range of high-quality cookware and negotiated for the endorsement of Le Cordon Bleu in its marketing campaigns.

The familiar Cordon Bleu brand increased the memorability of the new product to help build brand awareness for Tefal Integral, satisfying the first-level criterion for co-branding value creation. It also endowed the Integral brand with strong associations of culinary quality, particularly as the Cordon Bleu academy's chefs were shown to be using Integral cookware and endorsing its quality values, so meeting the criterion for second level-value creation. As Bob Boad points out in a later chapter, the CEO of Cordon Bleu was emphatic that

he did not see this as purely a financial transaction and was knowingly staking
his brand's values and reputation on the co-branded products.

This example highlights the importance of appropriate partner selection at the
higher levels of the value creation spectrum. Tefal was already a powerful and
reputable cookware brand and an ideal partner for Cordon Bleu, closely linked
to the brand's core features and values. Both partners were able to reinforce their
complementary brand reputations through the tie-up and stimulate increased
sales revenues for the co-branded products, so more value was created than
would have occurred if Tefal had partnered with, say, Chateau Rothschild for
quality or Citroën for reach.

Ingredient Co-Branding

The only distinct sub-category of co-branding that has been defined in the
marketing literature is our third level of value creation: Ingredient Branding, a
subject that Marc Smit explores in detail in Chapter 5 Ingredient branding is
typified by PC manufacturers with Intel, and Diet Coke with NutraSweet. The
rationale here is that a brand noted for the market-leading qualities of its product
supplies that item as a component of another branded product.

Both these examples illustrate that the second level of value creation, values
endorsement, is incorporated at the third level. An important part of the value
for IBM, Compaq or any other PC manufacturer of co-branding with Intel is
the reputation that Intel enjoys in the PC marketplace for the manufactured
quality and functional performance of its Pentium microprocessors. Quality and
performance are core values for the Intel Pentium brand and they migrate
through to the PC product.

The categorization of ingredient branding as a third level of value creation
is justified because there is an identifiable 'physical' component – the Intel
microchip or the NutraSweet ingredient or the VISA network – contained in the
'product' as sold to the customer. Without it, the value of the product would be
greatly diminished.

Cars provide a good illustration of the benefits of ingredient co-branding.
They are the most expensive branded purchases that most consumers ever make,
so the manufacturers want to attach strong emotional and intuitive values to
them in addition to their rational benefits and values. Many of the car
companies, particularly the global volume producers, have found that co-
branding deals enable them cost-effectively to reinforce particular brand images
and customize their products.

In the US, Ford uses Coach leather upholstery in its Lincoln cars and various
manufacturers, such as Lexus, use Bose audio products. In both these cases, the
use of these strongly branded ingredient items, associated in the consumer's

mind with high quality, is heavily promoted in the car's advertising to reaffirm the premium positioning of the vehicle. Similarly, Jaguar in the UK uses Connolly hide for its upholstery because of its quality brand image.

It is not only in the premium/luxury segment of the car-market that co-branding is used to reinforce particular values. In the sports saloon niche, several manufacturers use Recaro rally seats, partly because their seats have the right look and feel for the image they are trying to create and partly because the brand image of Recaro provides effective substantiation of the car's brand positioning. Similarly, Peugeot and Alfa-Romeo include a Pininfarina logo on their sports coupes, because of the long-standing reputation of that studio for leading-edge body design.

As you might expect, it is only the features that have always been considered of particular importance to the driver–owner, and which have spawned specialist-quality producers, that provide ingredient co-branding opportunities. No-one co-brands the make of steel used in the chassis, or most of the thousands of other parts that anonymously contribute to the vehicle's performance, because no sales or value benefit will accrue from so doing.

In summary, the essence of ingredient co-branding is that a manufacturer–provider wishing to convey focused messages about the attributes and values of their product uses and promotes branded components whose own brand image reinforces the desired attributes and values. The ingredient provider benefits by assuring sales volumes at the same time as reinforcing the attributes of their product brand. The assembler–manufacturer benefits by confirming the attributes and image of their product while sharing the marketing costs.

It is worth noting in passing that Monsanto and Intel reworked this logic in their respective deals with Coca-Cola and the PC manufacturers. Their product quality was well known but they were having difficulty in getting their products differentiated from other manufacturers'. They developed the strategy of branding their products strongly and then signing up co-branding deals with their customers, including joint promotion and heavy product advertising support. This approach enabled Intel and Monsanto to build product brands that achieved premium prices at the same time as increasing market share and stopped the commoditization of their industries.

Can the ingredient branding definition be applied to services as well as products? Examples are not generally quoted in the literature, but surely a premium hotel that put Bang and Olufsen televisions, the HBO movie channel and Crabtree & Evelyn toiletries in every room would be setting up the same type of co-branding relationship? Similarly, when Avis quotes in advertising that it uses GM cars, is that co-branding and are the cars 'ingredients' of a wider overall service proposition? With services, the boundary between endorsement and ingredient co-branding will always be somewhat blurred because the overall service is a complex mix of tangible and intangible elements, other benefits and the values embodied in the delivery.

Not surprisingly, the range of potential partners for an ingredient co-branding venture is very small in most markets. The product or service must lend itself to a senior–junior combination and there must be two strong brands already existing that can agree to co-brand. Alternatively, there must be a junior partner like Intel or NutraSweet, which is an essential component of the finished product/service, has the unique product features to sustain a brand and is willing to invest to build brand strength. In some cases, e.g. Intel, the ingredient brand may grow to be more valuable and powerful than the dominant brand appearing on the finished item. The ingredient brand may in such circumstances be the stronger motivator in the purchase decision.

Complementary Competence Co-Branding

At the fourth and highest level of co-branding, two powerful and complementary brands combine to produce a product that is more than the sum of the parts and relies on each partner committing a selection of its core skills and competencies to that product on an ongoing basis. Whereas ingredient co-branding requires the 'junior' partner to contribute a specific discrete component to the 'senior' partner's product, complementary competence co-branding involves a range of components, which may be tangible or intangible.

If this type of co-branding appears unusual, it is not so much because companies do not enter into such agreements as because they often establish a new brand, a formal alliance or a joint venture to manage this extensive commitment. Retailer co-branding provides excellent examples and this is covered extensively in Chapter 4.

A recent British example of complementary competence co-branding that appears to meet these criteria is the tie-up between Esso and Tesco Express to establish 24-hour mini-supermarkets at petrol stations. It repeats the formula pioneered by 7-Eleven with Mobil in the US and with Shell in Australia and extends it by using the brand of Britain's leading supermarket chain.

To this venture Esso brings its brand strength as one of the country's top three petrol retailers, its array of well-sited locations and its operational expertise in running petrol stations competitively. The benefits it would expect to reap are increased throughout and sales volume compared to operating the petrol station and shop on its own, plus increased brand loyalty from customers in return for the improved service its stations are able to provide.

For its part, Tesco Express brings the brand strength of the Tesco supermarket group, its knowledge of consumer buying-patterns and lifestyles, its purchasing expertise and market power, its distribution infrastructure and its operational expertise in running supermarkets.

Tesco has identified an opportunity to improve its market coverage and its overall service to its customer base by opening smaller 'convenience' stores in urban locations and has developed the Tesco Express sub-brand to describe this concept. Tesco Express stores are sited in convenient, high-traffic locations, are open for extended hours and focus on stocking the most frequently required merchandise. They are competing directly with the small independent corner stores which are more convenient than supermarkets but also much more expensive, as well as the 24-hour shops attached to many petrol stations.

For Tesco Express, the tie-up with Esso offers the benefit of rapid, high-profile expansion of its operating locations in prime sites, increasing customer awareness of the Tesco Express proposition and values. It also enables Tesco to achieve critical mass more quickly than it could have using stand-alone locations, so that it can fully exploit its distribution, purchasing and merchandising expertise and cost advantages. For example, about 40 per cent of the value of the typical customer's purchases is generally considered to be impulse purchases that were not planned in advance. The major chains like Tesco are expert in maximizing that spend through range selection, promotional offers and store layout, which corner stores and other petrol station shops are not.

The success of the Esso–Tesco Express co-branding venture relies on both parties contributing a high proportion of their core competencies and operational advantages to it on an ongoing basis, not just in designing and launching the concept. The value creation potential is high as the joint service can take significant market share through its attractive Esso locations and deliver very competitive operating costs through Tesco's retail efficiency.

The two brands are important elements of the proposition. Both Esso and Tesco convey such strong signals to the UK buying public with respect to their core offerings (petrol, supermarkets) that the partners would destroy value by creating a new brand to describe a venture so close to their core businesses. Not many companies enjoy such brand power in their markets, so they would have more difficulty in accelerating the growth of new services on the back of their brands and might prefer to set up a formal alliance with a new brand identity.

For this reason, identification of partners for complementary competence co-branding is likely to involve a broader commitment to co-operation, whether alliance, joint venture or co-branding. Which type of deal is eventually struck will depend on detailed analysis of the market characteristics and a shared decision about the best way to address that market. (See Chapter 7.)

Definitions for Other Types of Co-operation

Joint Promotions

By joint promotion we mean a short-term arrangement between two well-established consumer brands, such as McDonald's and Disney, for generating extra publicity and sales through combining the attractions of both brands. In the McDonald's–Disney example, there have been a number of occasions when merchandise and imagery evoking a current Disney film, such as Aladdin or Pocahontas, have been used on the standard range of McDonald's food and drinks. For Disney the promotion offers new sites and formats for publicising their latest movie to its target audience, while for McDonald's it refreshes their children's menu and offers a hook on which to hang topical advertising.

There are numerous other examples of such joint promotions in food and packaged goods. Typical characteristics are that they are short-term, less than six months, and they combine brands from different sectors. Often, as in the example above, the two brands address the same audience with non-competitive products, so the commercial incentive is to exploit the natural synergy between the brands and achieve greater audience impact at lower cost.

Sponsorship

Sponsorship deals typically involve an organization (often a charity) that has a strong and focused image and close relationships with a particular audience, given money by a company that wants to build a relationship with that audience. In return for the funding, the sponsored organization allows the sponsor to endorse their activities and gain publicity for so doing, the aim being that the positive image and values 'rub off' onto the sponsor.

There are large numbers of examples of sponsorship relationships, ranging from corporate brand sponsorships designed to convey 'good citizenship' and public spirit through to product brand sponsorships designed to convey focused image associations to defined target audiences. Successful examples of the former are Sainsbury's sponsorship of Comic Relief and Mars' sponsorship of the London Marathon.

Joint Ventures

Joint ventures, by contrast, are usually defined as long-term co-operative arrangements in which the branding issues are secondary to the operational opportunities. In many cases, the joint venture is established to enable two companies to enter new markets or launch new products to which both companies contribute.

A typical example of a joint venture is Symbian, the collaboration between Ericsson, Nokia, Motorola and Psion to create a new data transmission standard for mobile telephony. It is noteworthy that this group created a new name/brand to cover the joint venture but many others, such as General Electric and Snecma (jet engine manufacturers), co-operate using the venture partners' own brands. Joint ventures are most common in business-to-business markets, although brands are becoming increasingly influential.

As the examples illustrate, successful joint ventures are based around complementary skills or market access and allow the participants to reduce their own investment and competition exposure in launching a new product/service range. In Symbian, for instance, Ericsson, Motorola and Nokia contribute their technical expertise in mobile telephony handset design and manufacture, as well as their market reputations in this area. Psion contributes its expertise in electronic organizer design, software and manufacture. Working together, they can develop new products that integrate mobile telephony, data communication and personal organizer capabilities in one piece of hardware and allow the participants to rival anything that potential competitors like Microsoft might put together.

Joint ventures are usually set up with a management team seconded from both/all participant companies and funding allocated from both sides. A joint venture does not generally involve any exchange of parent company shares but often includes the creation of a new company, owned jointly (50:50 or 51:49 arrangements are typical) by the venture participants. It can last for many years, as demonstrated by the aero-engine combine mentioned.

Alliances

The terms alliance and joint venture are often used interchangeably in the management literature; inasmuch as they are definably different, the distinctions relate to marketing versus operations. While a joint venture is often undertaken for a long and capital intensive development project, an alliance is entered into principally for marketing reasons.

For example, a number of the world's leading airlines have now signed up for membership of either the Star Alliance (Air Canada, Lufthansa, SAS, Thai, United, Varig) or the oneworld alliance (American Airlines, British Airways, CanadianAir, Cathay, JAL, Qantas). In these partnerships, the airlines are all geographic substitutes for each other rather than providers of complementary services, as they would more likely be in a joint venture. There are some operational components to the alliance, for instance they are working to combine reservations and ticketing systems and will also lend and borrow planes for routes when required. Nevertheless, the majority of the alliance effort appears to be about marketing synergies.

What these global airline alliances allow is for each airline to pass their passengers from carrier to carrier within the alliance and potentially increase their customer loyalty by rewarding them for staying within the alliance on routes that their preferred carrier does not serve. By so doing they aim to improve their load factors and profitability, so a lot of effort is going into brand building, for both the alliance brand and the individual airline brands. These alliances are long-term arrangements, so they differ in that respect from joint promotions.

Why are alliances different from co-branding? The obvious difference is that they often involve the creation of a new 'master' brand (other examples are Global One, AT&T Unisource and the now defunct Concert in international telecoms) which is supported by the endorsement of the participants' brands. They are also potentially very long-term relationships with significant operational or technical elements as well as the marketing component. Like co-branding and joint ventures, they do not usually involve cross-ownership of equity.

The 'Essence' of Co-Branding

In its purest form co-branding embraces a collaborative venture designed to advance the interests of two (or more) parties in a considered, strategic fashion. Legally the parties concerned are independent entities and their intention is to create something new – a product, a service or an enterprise – the scope of which falls outside their individual areas of capability or expertise.

The creation of 'something new' is probably a defining issue, and thus we would probably include IBM–Intel, Diet Coke–NutraSweet and BP Mobil as examples of co-branding in perhaps its 'purest' form. Interdependence, too, is a defining issue. Each of these co-brands has acquired a measure of distinctiveness that is the product of the partners' brand personality, and is rather more than just a sum of the parts. It is difficult to see how this could be reproduced were one of the partners to drop out.

This definition, we feel, most closely reflects the 'spirit' of branding, which after all is fundamentally to do with innovation and distinctiveness; and while we would not arbitrarily exclude the numerous bank–credit card, airline–credit card, shop–charge card 'co-brands' we feel that these are possibly weaker examples of the 'genre'.

While this might seem to be a somewhat academic debate, defining co-branding in this way does have very important implications for the parties involved. We would suggest that the closer in character a co-brand is to a single brand (as defined above) the greater the necessity for the owners to manage their 'property' as if it were a single brand. This implies a strategic approach and has important legal, financial and management implications (these are discussed elsewhere in this book).

What About the Customer?

It may be useful now if we examine the issue of co-branding from unarguably the most important perspective: that of the consumer. It is legitimate to ask how consumers react when confronted by two familiar brand names presented in an unfamiliar context – in partnership. The union of BP and Mobil, if one can overcome the difficulty of accepting that two hitherto ancient rivals are now 'as one', does have a strong logic in that they have always operated in the same market. The union implied in the Delta SkyMiles Optima Card co-brand requires the consumer to reconcile two brands which, historically, have operated in different markets; here the binding logic is SkyMiles.

It is also pertinent to ask how consumers react when confronted by two familiar brand names presented in relation to a product or service with which neither is strongly associated. There are far fewer examples of such phenomena (logic dictates that alliances like these are extremely unlikely to take place) but a recent study by the American Marketing Association produced an interesting result. In a consumer survey on co-branding 80 per cent of the sample said that they would be likely to buy a digital imaging product co-branded by Sony and Eastman Kodak. However, of people told that the product was from Kodak alone, only 20 per cent said that they would buy it; similarly only 20 per cent said they would buy such a product from Sony. This indicates the weakness – or lack of credibility – of each firm separately, but a 'brand synergy' of potentially staggering dimensions. It is in this area, the area of technology collaborations, where the truly powerful co-brands of the future will develop; these we believe will produce the most enduring and valuable examples of the genre.

What can we conclude from this? Overwhelmingly there is a need to explain to consumers the rationale behind the co-branding venture and the benefits that the resulting product or service will supply. In introducing the GM–Visa card in the UK, for example, the partners had to set out clearly what were the advantages the consumer would enjoy over and above other cards; and also, critically, who were GM, a name unfamiliar in the UK where Vauxhall is the local General Motors subsidiary.

This then is the key to successful co-branding: the creation of a seamless logic that runs through the combined offer, the benefits of which can be readily understood by the consumer.

Some Preliminary Conclusions

The word 'preliminary' is used advisedly, as the use of co-branding is still very much in its infancy. The use of branding, however, is very well established and it is widely acknowledged that well-managed brands can become assets of considerable value. It seems appropriate, therefore, to start codifying rules for the management of co-brand projects, to ensure that the brands concerned emerge enhanced, rather than diminished, by the experience.

For many companies the use of co-branding is seen as tactical. Here the objective is to use the capabilities and reputation of a partner to enter a new market, market sector or country, and jointly make money. If the union develops into something more long-term, then so much the better; but the main intention is to carry through a specific business initiative designed to contribute positively to the bottom line

For other companies – particularly those in the technology sector where significant capital investment is required on both sides the returns on which may be some years away – the co-branding initiative will be more permanent. Irrespective of the duration of the relationship, however, the rules of good brand management should rigorously be applied to ensure that neither brand is weakened through association with the other and that, rather, an incremental benefit is derived.

In the co-branding literature, which is limited, it is salutary to see co-branding likened to marriage. 'There'll be hard feelings and problems' one exponent is quoted as saying 'and there needs to be an equal contribution and investment in the initiative.' 'It's just like marriage' quotes another 'sometimes you've got to work at it.' It is difficult to disagree with these sentiments and to an extent the marriage analogy, if somewhat trite, is appropriate. One can see the parallels: the careful selection and wooing of the marriage partner; the marriage contract; the consummation; the offspring; a happy and lasting union based on mutual compatibility, shared ideals and ambitions.

Unlike marriage, however, upon which the majority of people still embark in the hope that it will last, co-branding can be quite deliberately short-term in nature. This may have nothing to do with the compatibility of the partners or the success of the product, but everything to do with the duration of the opportunity. In such events, where all the emphasis is on maximizing the opportunity available, it is easy to see how careful brand-management practice can lapse. Thus when the relationship breaks up the partner brands can emerge damaged through neglect, and a relationship, which yielded short-term gains for both, found to be damaging to their long-term interests.

To pursue the analogy: with marriage 'à la mode' there is the underlying knowledge that if things do not work out then the arrangement can be terminated. So it is with co-branding. But what this entirely cynical perspective overlooks is the psychological and material damage that accrues, almost inevitably, to the former partners and their dependants.

In summary. co-branding – like marriage – is not something to be entered into unadvisedly, lightly or wantonly; it is a very serious business enterprise involving key assets of the partners concerned. The care of these assets over the course of the relationship – and beyond – must be uppermost in the minds of the partners, and the very first item on the 'heads of agreement'.

2 | Co-Branding Opportunities and Benefits

Bob Boad

B RAND OWNERS have found many different ways in which co-branding may be turned to advantage. For established brands it offers the opportunity to create an entirely new income stream or to boost sales of existing products and for new brands it may bring immediate credibility in a normally sceptical marketplace. Co-branding may reduce the need for costly investment in targeting new markets or be a means of overcoming non-financial barriers to entry, of gaining additional brand exposure, of reducing risk, of speeding investment payback, of facilitating price–profit maximization or of providing a novel way of communicating with the market. It can be used to gain short-term tactical advantage as well as for longer-term strategic purposes. In exceptional cases a brand may even be used in co-branding applications before it has been established as a separate entity in the marketplace and be the way in which its reputation is first established. Let us look in more detail at these advantages

Royalty Income

For manufacturers of products which are used as components or ingredients in the wares produced by their industrial customers, a co-branding deal offers the possibility of a new, secondary source of income. Instead of playing an anonymous and minor role in the final product offer, the manufacturer of the component–ingredient may be able to negotiate to receive additional payments if its brand is used upon the final product. In this way it can share with its partner the additional benefits which may be derived from co-branding, including receiving a proportion of the additional 'brand premium' by means of a royalty payment. To justify such royalties the owner of the 'ingredient brand' will need to convince its customer–partner that the overt use of the second brand will enhance the overall value of the offer and that incremental profits will more than compensate for the additional cost of royalty payments.

The owner of the 'ingredient brand' may have to make some marketing investment to communicate its brand values, both initially and on a continuing basis, to establish and maintain a strong reputation for its brand. This activity will need to reach both its immediate trade customers and the eventual consumers of the finished products which incorporate its ingredient–component and may require considerable funding and commitment. However, such a strategy offers the potential for tremendous long-term rewards for manufacturers of what might otherwise remain low-profile 'industrial' components or ingredients, as the examples discussed in Chapter 5 clearly demonstrate.

Sales Boost

The addition of a co-brand can significantly enhance the sales potential of a product or service, compared to a similar offer bearing only a single brand. Even strong and well-established brands can receive a significant boost by this means. For example, Ford Motor Company in the US introduced a special edition of its Explorer sports utility model, which also featured the successful outdoor clothing brand, Eddie Bauer. The co-branded 'Eddie Bauer' version reportedly outsold 'by head and shoulders' similarly equipped Explorer models that cost less.

Another clear example of the selling power of co-branding is to be found in the publishing field: a successful US cookery book written by the leading chef, Wayne Gisslen, and published by Wiley had already run to three editions. For the fourth edition the publisher decided to involve Le Cordon Bleu and co-brand the new volume with the culinary academy's logo. Sales increased dramatically as a result.

New Markets

One of the most obvious benefits of co-branding is that it may assist a brand owner to enter new markets. These may be new countries or regions which the brand owner feels unable to access by itself, or they may be additional sectors of existing geographical markets which it believes to be beyond reach without assistance. Even major brand owners may find the challenge of entering unfamiliar markets a daunting prospect and decide to enlist the support of a well-established local brand to maximize the chances of success.

An example of co-branding working in this way can be seen upon the 'Weight Watchers from Heinz' range of calorie-controlled food products. For the Weight Watchers International brand to enter directly the highly competitive market for prepared foods would have involved substantial investment and significant risks, even with its loyal following of active participants in its weight control programmes. Although Heinz may have considered the option of developing a range of diet products relying upon only its own brand it did have the handicap of being traditionally associated with canned and bottled foods. Therefore the established goodwill attaching to the famous Weight Watchers name and the high level of recognition and credibility which Weight Watchers International already possessed amongst the target audience for the range made co-branding an attractive proposition for both brands and enabled them to access the rapidly growing low-calorie foods sector.

When BP Amoco's lubricants business decided to enter the Indian market it did so by means of a joint venture with the leading Indian manufacturer Tata and the business decided to use both brands on its products. The co-branding worked well: Tata is a brand which is well-known to Indian consumers and trusted by them and although the average Indian may not have been familiar with BP Amoco because the company had not previously been very active in their country, influential businessmen and politicians knew of the energy company's reputation and technology and recognized the attractions of this powerful alliance. The co-branding allowed an attractive choice of marketing messages, utilizing the local trust in Tata and the technological resources of BP Amoco. Daya Chetty of TATA-BP Lubricants India explains 'TATA are a renowned manufacturer of automotive vehicles and BP Amoco are an accredited producer of fuels and lubricants. The fact that the respective products of the two companies were used in conjunction with one another meant that there was a natural relationship which underpinned the co-branding and provided strong credibility in the marketplace'.

Shyam Balasubramanian, General Manager (Marketing), TATA-BP Lubricants India, considers that there were four key factors which contributed to the successful co-branding in this venture:

> Firstly, the two companies were *complementary and not competing*. TATA was India's premier automotive manufacturer with a 70 per cent market share of heavy vehicles. BP's strengths came in further down the time cycle for the same consumer – in knowing how to keep that vehicle going.
>
> Secondly, the brands had almost *identical personality characteristics*. While BP was seen as a 'successful' and 'constructive' brand in the UK, TATA had an identical consumer perception in India. We were 'brand bridging' in the context of brands which had similar values and that eased the task.
>
> Thirdly, the companies brought *completely different skills to the table*. While BP brought with it international technology and international best practices in running a downstream operation in an efficient and environmentally safe manner, TATA brought with it an understanding of the local market, local consumer and local government regulations.

Lastly – at an executional level, the co-branding ensured *the brands were aligned vertically and not horizontally*. This ensured that consumers saw the company as a united, monolithic entity and not two separate companies working side by side.

We see the co-branding exercise as an extremely powerful alignment tool – taking the partners as well as the consumer beyond the conventional models of machine manufacturer/detergent and beauty salon/shampoos.

Additional Consumer Benefits

By using co-branding agreements businesses have been able to offer their customers greatly enhanced benefit packages, often at little additional cost to their mainstream operations. For example, a very wide range of companies have introduced credit or charge-card facilities: retailers, airlines, hotels, charities, oil companies and utilities such as telecommunications and gas companies, to name but a few. The exact motivation of the businesses participating in these deals varies from case to case, as do the benefits offered to the cardholders, but the agreements all enable a company that could not by itself offer its clients a widely accepted card to provide this valuable facility, and for the bank or finance house involved it permits access to an established and loyal customer base which would otherwise be difficult to reach.

Co-branding of credit and charge cards is a major growth market and it has created some unexpected partnerships, such as the all-Australian combination of Telstra (the national telecommunications company), Qantas (the national airline) and the local ANZ Bank who jointly operate a successful credit card. Despite the unusual combination of participants this has proved to be Australia's most successful locally developed example of co-branding to date. As usual with such co-branded cards, holders build up credits by using the card for their day-to-day purchases and they are able to redeem these by taking advantage of a range of attractive offers made available by Telstra and Qantas.

Investment Minimized

By using co-branding agreements a company can minimize the expenditure that is required to enter new markets or sectors. Sometimes the scale of investment that would be necessary to expand the horizons for a brand can exceed the financial resources of its owner but by carefully analysing both the strengths that the brand possesses and the opportunities that exist within the target sector, it may be possible to find an established brand which offers an ideal fit for a co-branding initiative. Even where a company can afford to acquire a new brand it may not be a cost-effective use of capital: in its 4 April 1998 issue *The Economist* commented that Quaker Oats spent $1.7 billion in taking over Snapple 'to force its way into the iced-tea business', whereas PepsiCo responded by simply forming an alliance with Lipton which, according to the report, was just as successful.

A good example of this type of co-branding involves the Harry Ramsden's brand, which was famous throughout the UK for its fish and chip restaurants and which had already achieved successful international expansion by means of restaurant franchising agreements in countries such as Singapore, Hong Kong and the Middle East. However, extending the brand in to the huge market for 'cook at home' fish fillets and prepared meals which are sold through supermarkets would have been risky and would have required substantial investment, a commitment that would have stretched the resources of this medium-sized business which was already investing heavily in its restaurant expansion programme. Their solution was instead to work with Young's, the leading seafood brand in the UK, and to evolve a co-branded offer which emphasizes features such as the high-quality batter approved by Harry Ramsden's.

This means of utilizing the enormous goodwill and reputation established by the branded restaurants helps Young's products to stand out as a unique and premium-quality product, compared to 'monobranded' fish products being marketed by their competitors. For the Harry Ramsden's brand the exposure in the supermarket sector and the increased consumer contact and familiarity with the brand helps to stimulate demand within its primary restaurant business.

Avoids Barriers to Entry

Co-branding also offers a means of overcoming non-financial obstacles to entering new markets or sectors. For example, where legislation limits the number of licensed operators, or where planning permission is required to establish a particular type of business activity, it may make commercial sense for a potential new entrant to embrace an established operator and propose a co-branded partnership or joint venture, rather than go it alone.

In the UK the supermarket operators were faced with a marketplace that was approaching saturation point – it was becoming increasingly difficult to establish additional premises, particularly obtaining planning permission for new out-of-town hypermarkets. Convenience stores were identified as one sector which offered considerable scope for further development but a new entrant would face huge investment costs and other difficulties if it tried to acquire an existing chain or attempted to create a new network from scratch.

Meanwhile, the major oil companies were keen to expand the role of the under-performing shops on their service station sites, to compensate for reduced margins on fuel sales, and they started to explore the potential for a partnership with a major supermarket brand. It was felt that involving an established supermarket operator would expand shop turnover significantly beyond that which an oil company could achieve with its own brand alone. The details of the various alliances that have been formed in this sector are discussed in Chapter 4.

Risk Reduction

One of the main attractions of co-branding is that it reduces the risk associated with entering new markets but it does not necessarily reduce the rewards. Launching new products is always a hazardous venture, particularly in new sectors or in unfamiliar territories, but by joining with, rather than competing against, an established player the risk of failure can be reduced. Uncertainty over customer reaction to a new brand in the sector is not the only concern – there is the possibility that existing brands may retaliate in some way against a new entrant (e.g. by a major advertising campaign or a price war) but they may find an enhanced, co-branded offer from a familiar rival more difficult to respond to as it will generally signal a product or service which is of higher perceived quality than previously, whilst retaining most of the positive qualities associated with the original.

The long-established White Castle chain of restaurants in the US was a strong brand in the market for hamburgers and when it decided to add a chicken offer to its range it considered creating a new in-house brand for the purpose. However concerns that the move might dilute the existing brand equity led to a decision instead to become a franchisee for the well-established Church's Chicken brand and to co-brand with this.

Quicker Returns

Co-branding offers the possibility of quicker returns on marketing investment than might be the case for similar expenditure on a new, single-branded offer. The synergy of two recognized brands, harnessed together, quickly translates into consumer response and may bring instant performance in the marketplace. In comparison, there will often be a slower build-up of recognition and consumer confidence, or the need for a greater investment in advertising and promotion, when consumers are exposed to a familiar brand appearing in a new sector as a result of a traditional 'brand extension'.

Price Premium

A carefully composed co-branding offer should command a premium above the prices enjoyed by equivalent products bearing only a single brand. The brand owner may be able to resist competitive pressure on price by stressing the quality benefits implicit in the co-branded product. A customer contemplating the purchase of an expensive carpet may well choose one which has a pile protected with Scotchgard brand protectant rather than an equivalent quality carpet which simply claims to have an unidentified stain-resistant finish applied to it. Customers may be prepared to pay more for a carpet treated with a well-known branded protectant.

Communicates High Product Quality

Co-branding can assist a manufacturer to communicate to consumers that their product is one which stands out from the pack of relatively undifferentiated and perhaps unexciting products. For example, the identification of Courvoisier VS Cognac as an ingredient in Sainsbury's Fresh Brandy Sauce leaves the customer in no doubt that it is of the highest possible quality. Such sauces are a traditional accompaniment to Christmas pudding and by highlighting the fact that theirs contained a premium brand cognac Sainsbury's were more easily able to convey the message that it was a superior-grade recipe in a market sector where there was otherwise little product differentiation.

Customer Reassurance

In some market sectors, for example expensive, high-tech products such as computers and hi-fi systems or products and services where health and safety is an issue, customers may be reluctant to try out new or unfamiliar brands. However, the appearance of a well-known mark in a co-branding role may provide adequate reassurance that the product or service merits a try. In some ways the co-brand is providing a similar type of comfort to that which consumers receive when they see the famous 'masterbrand' or 'house mark' of a leading manufacturer on a new product in its range – their reaction tends to be 'I may not have seen this particular product before but I recognize that brand and if they have a connection with it then I feel I can trust it'.

For the lesser-known brands of computer it is clearly a tremendous advantage to be able to gain consumer trust by displaying the 'Intel Inside' logo on their product. Would-be customers can immediately recognize and assess one important aspect of the product and can then move on to compare other aspects such as price and performance levels with greater confidence. The co-branding serves to remove some of the anxiety from the purchase decision for the consumer, assists the manufacturer of the finished product in getting distributors to accept the product on to their stock list and gives the owner of the 'ingredient brand' additional market reputation.

Users of stereo sound systems soon learned that tape decks which were co-branded with the Dolby logo offered significant benefits over most which were not, even some which bore primary brands that were household names. More recently the use of Dolby to co-brand 'surround sound' television receivers has provided additional customer reassurance, even where the set carries the brand of a famous manufacturer. In a close-run purchase decision the appearance of the Dolby co-brand will often win over a wavering customer who, by virtue of existing familiarity with the technical performance of Dolby's technology, brings to the current transaction some positive preconceptions that provide comfort in the risky situation of purchasing an expensive and unfamiliar piece of equipment.

Access to 'Leading-Edge' Technology

In fields such as computer hardware and software or Internet facilities, co-branding is growing at a phenomenal rate. The speed with which technology is advancing and the increasing specialization of participants make co-branding the only practical option for many businesses that offer products or services which are grafted on to existing systems and technologies.

According to Todd Bontemps, Trademark Attorney with Cooley Godward, a law firm in Palo Alto, California who have several clients involved in co-branding ventures:

> The current trend in much of the high-tech industry is to 'layer' one company's technology on to another's to achieve a more desirable end product. And, as the number of speciality or niche technology companies increases so too do the opportunities to join or combine independently owned and developed technology and know-how. As a result, co-branding is often a convenient way for each party to identify its respective contribution to the consumer – whether to signify a particular chip or software program inside a computer, to certify a product has met a certain level of operating compatibility, or to identify which aspect of a single Internet website was produced by whom. For example, the 'search' technology utilised in the site and the site's content (text, graphics, sounds, etc.) may be owned by entities other than the owner of the site itself! Many companies use co-branding as a way not only to identify and distinguish their respective technology but also to market the attractiveness of their own technology by associating it and their related trademark with another company's brand.

The phenomenal success of companies such as Intel (with their 'Intel Inside' mark) and Microsoft (with their 'Designed for Microsoft Windows 98' mark), both of which have achieved high-profile co-branding on computers even though the brands primarily relate to microprocessors and software respectively, have encouraged many other companies to adopt co-branding as the route to successful marketing in high-tech industries. In some sectors co-branding has become the norm rather than the exception.

Sun Microsystems, Inc. with its Java brand technologies is another active and successful co-brander. The Java concept was born when a small group of Sun engineers decided to tackle the problem of getting the digital systems incorporated in countless modern devices to work together and integrate. Systems developers and end-users both enjoy the benefits of Java technology and it has led to a huge variety of new products, particularly in relation to its Internet applications which include facilitating the distribution of software quickly and inexpensively, even offering the potential for 'pay per use' charging instead of traditional fixed-price sales. The nature of the Sun's Java business makes it an obvious candidate for co-branding. For example, the 'Java Compatible' logo is licensed for use in relation to products which have passed tests laid down by Sun and otherwise comply with certain compatibility and certification requirements, and it is seen upon a rapidly expanding range of software.

Cisco Systems, Inc. is another tremendously successful co-brander and its 'Cisco Powered Network' logo is an increasingly common sight, although of the almost 10 000 service providers in the world, only 1 per cent have qualified for the Cisco Powered Network programme. Virtually all Internet traffic already travels across Cisco equipment but to boost awareness of their brand they have undertaken a major international marketing programme aimed at end-users. The advertising informs businesses of the benefits of Cisco's technology and encourages them to choose a service provider who makes use of it, but for many customers the reassurance offered by the appearance of the Cisco co-brand is of greater importance. Cisco also achieves strengthened relationships with the service providers who are members of the programme and enjoy benefits of the type described below under 'Trade Customer Relations'.

According to Mike Heller, Program Manager of Cisco Powered Network:

> the goal for the program is to strengthen our relationships with key network service providers by creating a 'win-win' environment. By promoting the virtues of our 'ingredient brand' (reliability, security, scalability, dependability, interoperability) generally, and by various efforts to refer end-user customers to 'members' of the program (whether directly at trade shows, or indirectly by media advertising), Cisco seeks to increase demand for the services of such members. Because of our dominant position in the Enterprise networking marketplace, Fortune 1000-type users are

likely to already be Cisco customers and the program attempts to extend the credibility and confidence of our customers across members of the Cisco Powered Network program. Each service provider in the program has a Program Manager assigned to them who acts as a liaison to various Cisco marketing resources and co-ordinates the implementation of joint marketing programs such as seminars, trade show promotions, direct mail, event sponsorships, Web ads and links, etc.

Market Priming

Occasionally co-branding may be used to help establish an entirely new brand and be used as the preliminary stage of a longer-term marketing strategy, rather than be utilized as a means of enhancing the returns for an already successful brand. The co-branding is used to gain consumer recognition for the new brand and once this has been established the brand can then be used alone, perhaps in a different sector. This strategy may be particularly attractive as a means of challenging a market sector that is relatively mature, with several strong established brands.

Monsanto used this technique to great effect in launching NutraSweet. Rather than try to establish this innovative sweetener directly in the market, Monsanto first used it as an 'ingredient name' in their established Equal brand sweetener. Then they targeted established confectionery brands such as Diet Coke cola and Wrigley's Extra chewing gum and convinced the manufacturers that their product had taste advantages over saccharin and other existing sweeteners but, rather than allowing it to become another anonymous ingredient, Monsanto persuaded the manufacturers that there were benefits to be derived from co-branding, with NutraSweet being identified in on-pack flashes.

A key element in their strategy was the advertising which Monsanto decided to undertake to familiarize consumers with the merits of NutraSweet as this firmly underpinned the co-branding activity: it not only signalled a commitment to develop the brand but reassured the partners that the co-branding held advantages for them as the advertising encouraged consumers to actively seek out products which contained the ingredient. Tremendous goodwill was created for NutraSweet by being utilized alongside some of the world's most valuable brands and eventually it became the expected standard in the low-calorie soft drinks market as other leading brands also adopted it as a co-brand.

So successful was the NutraSweet strategy that it is credited with being the role model adopted – and adapted – by Intel in establishing their microprocessors.*

---

* See Stephanie Thompson, 'Brand Buddies' in *Brandweek* 39 (8), 22–30 (23 February 1998; ISSN 1064–4318).

Reinforcement of Advertising Messages

Advertising undertaken by the owner of an 'ingredient brand' which is aimed at the end-users of the completed product incorporating the ingredient or component should help to reinforce the promotional activity undertaken by the manufacturer of the finished item.

Such advertising may also permit the advertising of the finished product to concentrate on other features of its offer without needing to commit effort to communicating the particular benefits of the ingredient or component. For example, a relatively unknown manufacturer of computers which incorporate Intel processors can concentrate on informing its customers about other features of its product design or back-up service without needing to explain the benefits of the processor because Intel's own advertising will have tackled that aspect.

Brand Exposure

This can be a very valuable advantage for some brand owners who would otherwise be faced with a low-profile image for their brand. Co-branding can also bring such brand owners some valuable secondary benefits, including improved access to finance resulting from the enhanced recognition within the investment and finance community.

According to Todd Bontemps:

> Co-branding can offer many high-tech 'non end-user' companies, such as component manufacturers, tremendous brand exposure advantages. For example, if I sell imaging chips for digital cameras and I persuade a camera manufacturer which uses my chip to display my chip trademark on the camera itself as well as on the outside of the retail packaging, I am receiving infinitely more brand exposure compared to only labelling the minuscule chip hidden inside the camera or displaying my trademark in written technical or product collateral material included with the operating manual. For the technology niche player a true measure of both a successful business and a successful brand is when the distinguishing technology component serves as the 'tie-breaker' for the wavering consumer: 'I bought camera A instead of camera B because A has the X chip'. Once the consumer reaction occurs, every camera manufacturer will want to prominently display the X chip mark on their packaging.

Consumer Interest

In well-established or crowded market sectors co-branding can be an effective way of achieving product differentiation and attracting consumer interest. For example, in the US, food manufacturer Pillsbury wanted to introduce some turkey-based soups and its market research revealed that co-branding with the mark of a well-known turkey producer would add customer interest. Pillsbury conducted surveys to discover which turkey brand appealed most to consumers and settled upon the Hillshire Farm brand belonging to the Sara Lee group.*

In a mature market sector, such as that for bathroom towels, finding fresh ideas is always a tough challenge. However, Christy's, the Courtaulds subsidiary and current UK market leader in this sector, decided that their new range of bath and beach towels featuring wild animals such as tigers, zebras and elephants would prove even more popular if they were co-branded with the logo of the World Wide Fund For Nature (WWF). After careful examination of the proposal the conservation organization was pleased to enter into such an agreement. Graham Minton, Senior Marketing Executive of WWF reports 'We are delighted to be working so closely with Christy's, whose practice of using bleach with no chlorine and no heavy metals fits well with WWF's commitment to supporting products that use more environmentally friendly practices.'

Luxury cruise operator Silversea decided to join with Le Cordon Bleu culinary academy and add a co-branded offer to its range of holidays. Passengers are not only treated to Epicurean delights prepared by Master Chefs from Le Cordon Bleu but are also able to enjoy cookery demonstrations, wine tastings and seminars on the French art of table-setting. These features add considerably to the attraction of the co-branded voyages and they tend to sell out especially quickly.

Adding Distinctiveness to Diluted Product Get-ups

Where a trade dress or get-up has become commonplace in a market sector and consumers rely upon it to signal a particular type of product or service, the use of a co-brand can enable a product or service to distinguish itself from its 'lookalike' rivals, whilst still retaining the benefits of instant recognition and association with the relevant product or service sector. Whilst care must be taken to ensure that the co-branding does not itself turn a distinctive mark into a generic term that is free for all to use (see Chapter 3 and 6 for a further discussion of this issue) it may represent a valuable way to 'stand out from the crowd' in a sector that has an established 'look' which is non-proprietary.

---

* See *Brandweek*, ibid.

Special Promotions

Producers of fast-moving consumer goods will often produce seasonal variants of their standard products with distinctive packaging to catch consumer attention at particular times of the year – such as summer or Christmas – or they will produce a special limited-edition version of their product which has a finite production run. Some have found co-branding to be the ideal foundation for a short-term promotional version of their regular product. In the UK, Golden Wonder potato crisps introduced a co-branded turkey and Paxo stuffing flavour to boost sales during the Christmas season. The Christmas period is an important one for sales of Paxo stuffing and in addition to the direct returns earned by the crisps, the co-branding offered useful additional exposure for the brand during this critical time. The co-branded crisps provided supplementary customer contact for the Paxo brand (and hence prompts for the purchase of the primary line of stuffing) in additional sections of supermarkets and fresh exposure opportunities in outlets where the brand would not normally be seen, such as cafeterias and snack bars.

Trade Customer Relations

The owner of a strong brand can, by licensing it to an important customer for use in a co-branding venture, reinforce the relationship and more securely 'tie in' the customer to a long-term purchasing commitment. Once consumers get used to seeing the co-branding on a product they may be a force for continuity in the arrangements. In the US, Kellogg was a major customer of ConAgra for commodity grains and this was reported to be a factor in the decision to license Kellogg to use ConAgra's valuable Healthy Choice brand upon breakfast cereal.

Enhancing of Brand Value

One of the benefits of co-branding activity may be to increase the worth of a brand which has been so licensed – for example exposure in additional market sectors as a result of the co-branding initiative may result in a significant uplift in its open-market value. In the case mentioned above, where ConAgra's Healthy Choice brand was licensed to Kellogg in the breakfast cereal sector, the high-profile consumer usage is likely to have increased the worth of the brand beyond that which it had as a result of its original use in trade circles.

However, it must be recognized that inappropriate or unsuccessful co-branding can have a negative effect on the overall value of a brand, so care must be taken in choosing the opportunities.

Assimilation of Positive Values from Partner Brand

In recent years charities have adopted more imaginative strategies for fund-raising and co-branding can offer them opportunities for attractive commercial developments. Increasingly large companies are recognizing that they have environmental and social responsibilities, in addition to the traditional financial responsibilities owed to their shareholders, and the positive values associated with a well-known charity can bring some worthwhile benefits for a business which is seeking to create a 'warmer, friendlier' image with consumers. According to Business in the Community, 86 per cent of people would be more likely to buy a product that was linked to a charity.

One charity which has established a significant programme of co-branding is the World Wide Fund For Nature (WWF), the world's largest independent conservation organization. The WWF's Panda logo is one of the best recognized brands in the world, scoring 77 per cent prompted awareness in tests carried out in the UK,* and WWF have entered into co-branding agreements for a wide range of products and services which include recycled paper, wall-coverings, towels, neckties and credit cards. The charity is naturally very selective about its partners in such ventures and a commitment to environmental improvement is required but a pragmatic approach is taken, with commercial viability being balanced alongside environmental responsibility.

Stephen Bellingham, Managing Director of Fellowes Manufacturing, is very satisfied with the results of the co-branding agreement which his company has signed with WWF, enabling them to launch a unique 'Panda' range of recycled paper products which has enjoyed great success. He comments: 'The link with WWF has added credibility to our environmental policy and we are delighted that the sales generated have in turn helped WWF with its own programmes.'

Communication Opportunities

Co-branding ventures offer a brand owner the chance to communicate with customers of its partner brand, for example, on packaging materials or literature associated with co-branded services. For instance, the Weight Watchers club took advantage of the opportunity to include on the labels of its co-branded range with Heinz details of how to contact them and participate in their weight-loss programme.

The co-branding partnership with Christy towels, mentioned previously, enables the World Wide Fund For Nature (WWF) to promote its work and

---

* *Source:* UK market research company, MORI.

provides fundraising opportunities in the 40 Christy concession shops across the UK. Similarly, WWF's agreement with Tie Rack, a specialist designer and retailer of ties, scarves, clothing and accessories, offers them a global audience for their conservation messages by utilizing Tie Rack's 450 outlets in 31 countries. WWF also benefits by receiving worthwhile financial returns from the sale of the co-branded products, all of which are produced in accordance with Tie Rack's policy of not using heavy metals in printing and incorporating recycled fibres into most of its packaging.

Retailer Collaboration

Total and Alldays were the first in the UK to test the concept of exposing a supermarket brand on an oil company forecourt and their partnership has been considered a particularly successful example. The later deal between BP Amoco and Safeway attracted special interest because of the size of the partner companies, even though they decided to begin with only seven co-branded pilot sites, using the BP brand for the forecourt offer and the Safeway brand for the stores. The interior of the stores were reworked, using a design and a range of stock that differed considerably from that which motorists had come to expect in shops on BP service stations. The turnover and profitability of the pilot sites increased significantly and quickly convinced the partners to extend the programme to a network of more than 100 stores.

More recently Exxon, operator of the UK's largest service station network, and Tesco, the largest UK supermarket company, announced plans for a similar joint network. They will feature Tesco Express convenience stores alongside Esso branded forecourts, although the companies have vowed to continue to compete head-on elsewhere as Tesco is a significant player on its own behalf in the fuel sector and has service stations established at many of its larger supermarket sites.

Other similar alliances in the UK include Elf joining up with Somerfield and the format has also been adopted elsewhere in the world as major oil companies seek to work their retail assets harder and supermarkets seek new avenues for growth. For example, in New Zealand BP Amoco has joined with leading supermarket operator Woolworths, in that country's first such venture. Each party holds a 50 per cent stake in the venture and Fiona MacLeod, Retail Strategy Manager of BP New Zealand, explains that management from both companies researched the concept in the UK, Portugal and Australia before finalizing the details and they believe it will offer their customers the most advanced model in the world. Starting with only two pilot sites in order to evaluate the suitability of the concept for the New Zealand market they will expand the chain if the preliminary results are encouraging. 'This initiative is designed to meet people's changing needs. As lifestyles and shopping habits change, today's time-hungry customers are looking for convenience, speed and service at supermarket prices' says BP New Zealand Managing Director, Greg Larsen. The stores will open 24 hours a day and Andrew Davidson, Chief Executive of Woolworths, comments that the really great thing about the partnership is that it gives customers a new choice of how and when they shop: 'From now on consumers will be able to buy petrol and do their supermarket shopping quickly in one spot and pay only supermarket prices. That's what makes this different. It is an entirely new shopping choice.'

It is ironic that it was the entry of supermarkets into the petrol market and the subsequent erosion of profit margins on the traditional fuel sales that eventually led to the oil companies inviting these new competitors to join with them in developing the substantial real estate assets represented by their service station stores. The subject of retailer co-branding is considered in greater detail in Chapter 4.

In Conclusion

These, then, are the main opportunities offered by co-branding and the benefits that can accrue. Whilst no co-branding prospect can expect to realize all of these benefits, every such deal ought to be offering the partners involved in it at least one of them, otherwise the exercise is unlikely to be justified. Clearly, co-branding can be a powerful and versatile tool, offering major strategic and financial advantages to those who 'get it right'– but it is not without risk. The next chapter seeks to identify the problems that can arise.

3 | The Risks and Pitfalls of Co-Branding

Bob Boad

CO-BRANDING may not be all plain sailing and you should not approach it with unrealistic expectations of high rewards for little investment or effort. There are considerable risks to your brand's reputation if you choose the wrong partner brand or if your partner brand suffers a setback in the marketplace or receives bad publicity for some reason. As with selecting a partner in any other business context, it pays to make sure that you have thoroughly investigated their background and their values to minimize the risk of unexpected problems. It may be wise to ensure that the co-branding agreement provides for the possibility of termination in the event that the partner brand or the co-branded product suffers a serious reputation problem, to minimize the possibility of knock-on damage to your own brand. In this chapter we examine some of these risks and pitfalls.

Financial Greed

Perhaps the greatest risk that arises in relation to co-branding is to focus too much on the immediate monetary rewards that the deal may appear to offer. The co-branding activity must be viewed as something that contributes to the growth of the long-term brand value, not as a way to make a 'fast buck' and cash in on the existing goodwill by exposing the brand to risks as part of a questionable venture.

Even where a wise choice of co-branding project has been made, it will often be sensible for the brand owners to accept a modest return in the early stages, to allow a reasonable proportion of the profits to be re-invested in building up the co-branded product or service. A fair split of the profits is also necessary because only by allowing the partner to earn a reasonable reward from the project can it be motivated to develop the co-branding as a long-term relationship.

Le Cordon Bleu is the world's leading culinary academy and it has entered into a number of successful co-branding ventures with carefully chosen partners in Europe, Japan, Australia and the Americas. According to André Cointreau, President and CEO of the company:

> The potential size of the royalty cheque should not be the primary consideration when evaluating a co-branding opportunity. A careful match of our brand values with those of a partner who shares a similar focus on long-term brand development, and making sure the business sector is appropriate for us, are where we place the emphasis. If a brand owner has doubts that a co-branding opportunity or a potential partner is appropriate then the correct course of action is to decline the invitation to participate. Like marriage there is only one chance to be the first partner and the commitment should not be undertaken lightly just because it is not the brand owner's primary business. If the co-branding partner is ill-suited and there are problems with the venture then the value and credibility of your brand may be compromised and not just in that sector.

Incompatible Corporate Personalities

Businesses have personalities and like humans they do not always find the characters of others to their liking. The attitudes and values of a proposed co-branding partner may differ significantly from those of your own company and the potential for such divergence to cause friction should not be underestimated. Conflicts in relation to day-to-day matters, such as dealing with customer complaints, can prove just as big an irritant as disputes over broader policy issues, such as environmental concerns.

If your company is one which likes to have complete control of a venture then it will find co-branding a difficult concept and may prefer to stick to simple brand extensions or diversifications which involve only brands it owns.

Over-extended Brand Franchise

There have been many failed attempts to extend the use of successful brands to new categories of products or services. The failure can often be attributed to over-ambitious brand owners, attempting to stretch their brand equity across to sectors that are too far removed from the field where the brand has established its reputation. The same principle applies to decisions involving the extension of brands to new products or services by means of co-branding activity – the brand owner must be satisfied that consumers will respond positively to the brand in its new role and that they will feel it offers them some worthwhile benefits.

In Japan, Le Cordon Bleu culinary academy was offered a potentially lucrative co-branding opportunity with a leading marketer of coffee. After careful consideration of all of the implications they declined it because of concerns about the appropriateness of their brand, and in particular the expertise and values that it represents, being over-extended into that sector of the grocery market.

However, they had no such qualms about entering into an agreement with Nippon Ham, Japan's fourth largest food manufacturer, for the marketing of a co-branded range of pâtés, terrines and speciality pre-cooked dishes. André Cointreau, President of Le Cordon Bleu, explains:

> The arrangements are carefully controlled. We supply all of the recipes used for the co-branded items and no new products being added to the range without our prior testing and approval. Similarly, the recent co-branding agreement between Le Cordon Bleu and Tefal relating to the new high-quality Integral range of cookware arose from a common bond in that the cookware is used by our chefs in their day-to-day activity. This is therefore much more than a mere endorsement – it is co-branding of a product range upon which Le Cordon Bleu and Tefal are both prepared to stake their reputations.

Partner Brand Repositioning

If the owner of a brand decides to alter the positioning or strategy relating to the brand in its primary market sector, then this may represent a problem for its partner in a co-branding venture. It is vital that the overall brand strategies remain compatible and that both parties remain comfortable with the broader aspects of their partner's marketing and the other activities that may reflect upon the associate brand's image.

The parties may wish to provide in the agreement that the parties will discuss in advance any plans for a significant repositioning of either brand. In extreme cases one party may feel that the changes being contemplated by the other are so fundamental that it wishes to terminate the co-branding arrangements and so it may also be prudent to provide for such an eventuality in the agreement.

Change in Financial Status of Partner

If one brand owner becomes bankrupt or suffers some other financial crisis which renders it unable to proceed with its share of planned investment in the co-branding venture, then the other party may feel it is necessary to end the relationship or significantly restructure the arrangements and division of the returns. Ideally the agreement should provide for this, although care needs to be taken to ensure that such a step is permissible, as in some countries it may be illegal to terminate a deal in certain circumstances because the continued operation of the business under the agreement may offer the Receiver the best hope of finding a buyer for the company or of achieving a recovery and paying off the creditors.

Failure to Meet Targets

Where one of the partners finds that the co-branded activity fails to meet its financial projections or other goals there is the risk that it will force a summary termination of the agreement and thereby cause embarrassment or difficulties for the other party who may be left with disappointed customers who wished to continue purchasing the co-branded product or service. The co-branded credit card issued in the US by Price Chopper supermarkets and M&T Bank failed to live up to the bank's expectations because too many shoppers paid off their balances each month and did not incur any interest charges. This led M&T to terminate the arrangement.

Takeovers and Mergers

If one of the parties involved in a co-branding venture is taken over or enters into a merger this can have serious implications for the co-branding relationship and in some cases may lead to the immediate termination of the deal. Again it may be wise to anticipate such an eventuality and provide in the agreement between the parties for the option summarily to terminate in such circumstances, subject to the usual confirmation that such a clause is legal in the relevant jurisdiction. For example, a merger may leave a company with two very similar co-branding deals, as happened when Bank One and First Chicago joined up, resulting in the merged bank having two similar co-branding deals, one with British Airways and the other with United Airlines.

Changes in Market Attitudes

We live in an age when the tastes and opinions of society can change with surprising rapidity. A brand owner will be well placed to gauge changes in consumer attitudes in relation to its primary products or services and react accordingly. However, it may be easier to overlook or be slow to react to shifts in public opinion that relate to a co-branding venture which is not a mainstream business for the brand. This may result in a consumer backlash that threatens the overall brand image.

Back in 1987 Harley-Davidson licensed Loews Corporation's Lorillard subsidiary to use the Harley-Davidson brand upon cigarettes. The subsequent change in public opinion on smoking was reported to have led to increasing public relations difficulties for Harley-Davidson and it decided to terminate the license to avoid further controversy.

Creation of a Single 'Hybrid' Brand

If customers start to see the two brands as a single hybrid brand then this should be recognized as a major problem requiring urgent action to try to remedy the situation. The exact course of action will depend upon the particular circumstances but steps to try to correct the misconception will certainly be required if the continuing validity of the brands is not to be placed at risk. For example, joining two brand names together by having one prefixing the other, or superimposing one logo on top of the other, are particularly risky practices and can easily lead to the belief that the marks consolidated in this way constitute a single brand.

Loss of Exclusivity for Brand Features

Beware carry-over of your distinctive brand livery on to your partner's independent marketing activities via the co-branding activity or you could end up with diluted or shared rights to what started out as a strong and distinctive get-up (trade dress) used exclusively by yourself. The value of distinctive labels, devices, colour combinations, packaging shapes, advertising themes and slogans, vehicle liveries, staff uniforms, or other 'marketing indicia' should not be underestimated and they should be properly controlled and licensed for use only in relation to the co-branded activities and only in the exact manner dictated by their owner. The partner must be prohibited from deviating from the rules for use and be prevented from utilizing them on other products or services which do not form part of the co-branded range.

Increased Risk of 'Lookalikes'

In some market sectors, such as over-the-counter pharmaceuticals, there is a trend towards producing co-branded products that feature a manufacturer's well-known brand together with the mark of the large retailer or wholesaler who is selling it. According to a report in *Chemist & Druggist* on 16 August 1997 it is becoming increasingly common for multiple retailers to 'commission' manufacturers of established branded medicines to produce co-branded packs for their exclusive use, citing the Co-Op's version of Distalgesic and the Tenormin pack produced specially for Unichem as examples of such products that were then available in the UK market.

However, unless great care is taken, such an arrangement may expose the manufacturer to an increased risk of 'lookalike' packs subsequently appearing. After a period of time, during which the appearance of the co-branded pack becomes well known to consumers, the retailer or wholesaler may be tempted to substitute a rival product bearing a similar-looking pack. Unless the manufacturer has taken care not to compromise its position it may be in a weakened position to challenge such imitation products.

To be best placed to deal effectively with such a development, the manufacturer should ensure that it uses a distinctive get-up (trade dress) for its original product packaging, has registered this as a trademark, has insisted upon continuing to use this original pack livery for the co-branded product (apart from a modest on-pack 'flash' indicating the retailer–wholesaler's brand) and has ensured that the retailing or wholesaling partner formally acknowledges that the get-up, as well as the manufacturer's brand name, is only licensed for use upon the co-branded product and remains the exclusive property of the manufacturer. Failure to attend to these points could result in ambiguity over the ownership of the get-up for the co-branded product and this could make it difficult for the manufacturer to challenge a new 'lookalike' product that utilizes a similar pack get-up, particularly if the former retailing or wholesaling partner is 'commissioning' its production and claiming shared ownership of the copyright or other intellectual property rights.

Degeneration of a Trademark into a Generic Term

In extreme circumstances a brand owner may lose the exclusive right to use a trademark as a result of careless co-branding activity. A trademark is by definition associated exclusively with the goods and services of a single proprietor and it indicates the trade source of same. Where the mark ceases to function in this way as a 'badge of origin' it is likely to have become generic and instead be used to describe a type or quality of product or service. In these circumstances any registration of the mark is liable to be cancelled and the mark be declared free for all to use. This fate can befall not only word marks but also other types of mark such as colour schemes or packaging get-up and the consequences can be disastrous for the brand owner.

Co-branding activity presents such a risk for brand owners unless they take great care to control the situation. For example, poorly managed projects to produce retailer or wholesaler co-branded versions of a product, of the type described under the previous heading, can easily lead to such a situation. Evidence that customers and the trade view the mark as indistinctive or descriptive, starts to build up and a competitor may then be tempted to adopt the mark itself and apply to have any registration of it cancelled.

DuPont, owner of the famous Lycra brand for spandex stretch yarn, recognized that its valued brand was at risk through a widespread misunderstanding of the status of the word. A major problem for DuPont was that its product was used as an ingredient by manufacturers of fabrics and clothing which meant that it had little direct control over the way in which these customers presented the mark upon their labels and in their advertisements. DuPont decided that preventive action was called for to remove the risk of losing exclusive rights to the mark as a result of misuse and it embarked upon a major programme to educate manufacturers and retailers, along with journalists and even its own employees, on the correct way to use the brand name. It adopted a friendly, positive and informative approach, in contrast to the usual threatening stance adopted by many other brand owners, and the programme was judged a major success in stemming the threat to the validity of the brand.

Brand Separation

Dismantling the co-branding and re-establishing your brand on a stand-alone basis can be just as difficult as maximizing the synergy of using the two brands together in the first place: a co-branded product or service may have enormous recognition in the marketplace and a value which does not immediately evaporate. This is particularly true if the co-branding has been the sole or main exposure for one or both of the brands in that country. Termination of the sale of the co-branded product or service may also tempt unscrupulous competitors to cash in with an imitation of the co-branded offer, especially if neither partner continues to offer a replacement in the same market sector. For several decades the successful Shell-Mex & BP joint venture used both of the famous brands in relation to its distribution and marketing of petroleum products and customers got used to seeing them together on road tankers, railway wagons and on service station forecourts in many countries. Although the venture was dissolved in 1976 and since that date both companies have marketed their products independently, for some years following the termination a small proportion of the public, particularly older customers who had grown familiar with the relationship over many years, mistakenly continued to believe there was some sort of connection between these two companies.

Disciplined Trademark Use is Vital

The agreements made between the parties should provide for the controlled use of the brands and ideally a Visual Standards manual containing rules for their correct use should be produced. Details such as prohibiting the juxtaposition of the brands and setting out any statements to accompany them on packs, in ads, etc. are essential. Both partners must abide by the rules and there has to be trust and mutual respect between them, as in any successful partnership.

Co-branding activity has great potential to create confusion in the mind of the consumer if the result of carelessly using two brands on a single product or service is that a muddled message comes across. However, if the respective roles of the two brands are communicated clearly then the customer benefits by deriving only additional reassurance from the presence of the second brand. In Chapter 6 there are some guidelines for the proper use of two brands together and also some advice on the risks associated with confusion over status and ownership of the marks used for co-branding activity.

Sibling Brand Incompatibility

Where two brands have common ownership there may be a loss of objectivity about how well suited they are for co-branding purposes. There may be a reluctance to evaluate the potential co-branding operation with the same rigour that would be applied if an unrelated brand proposed a similar deal yet the opportunity cost for the brands remains the same regardless of their shared proprietorship. It will not benefit them if they are forced into inappropriate co-branding situations.

For over twenty years Heinz has owned Weight Watchers and it has used the brand successfully on a range of co-branded reduced-calorie foods. It is a classic example of creating synergy from two in-house brands.

The Burger King and Häagen-Dazs brands both belong to the same group of companies but efforts to market the brands jointly have not been particularly successful because of different customer profiles. Fortunately the management recognized this from its monitoring and so they have concentrated on growing the brands independently.

Anti-Trust and Other Legal Problems

Co-branding has the potential to cause brand owners a variety of legal problems which might not arise in connection with 'monobranded' marketing activities. These are discussed in greater detail in Chapter 6.

In Conclusion

This chapter, pointing out some of the risks and pitfalls of co-branding, is somewhat shorter than the last which considered the opportunities and benefits. The reason that this should be so is not difficult to explain. Co-branding is a relatively new subject; its successes are well known, its failures buried in decent obscurity. No famous brand we know of has yet been brought down through an incautious liaison, but the pace and scope of co-branding is increasing fast and with it the risks and pitfalls. Success will only come to those companies who understand and acknowledge these dangers and manage them – ignoring the threats only makes them more likely to occur.

4 | Co-Branding – a Retailer's Opportunity

Mark Linnell

Rᴇᴛᴀɪʟᴇʀs are big business. Their brands are even bigger. They position carefully selected ranges of goods and services and develop interesting and exciting promotions to reap the rewards from loyal customers. If they get it right, these customers return to buy more, over and over again. New product development is expensive and only the largest companies have the funds to invest. By building bigger brands for themselves they have had to look at doing business with other brands from different and, in some cases, competitive categories to enhance the vitality and the dynamism of their offers. Staying on top is tough; increasing the lead is tougher, so why not get help from another leader?

It is not just retailers who are creating alliances to strengthen their consumer marketing offers. Utilities, telecommunications and computer companies have been building strategic alliances for a number of years. Their goals have been to improve their product's point of difference by adding a new innovative ingredient to their customer offer. For retailers, forming alliances, beyond the straightforward stocking of a new product on their shelves, has taken a new turn. Their aim is to maximize their brand strengths or reduce their weaknesses by adding to their offers. Asda, for example, in introducing clothing, developed a co-brand in George. George Davies, the man credited with designing the Next chain's style, was introduced to Asda. Asda's consumers trusted their supermarket and when clothing was added a further level of trust and interest was delivered in the form of the George brand.

Marks & Spencer's brand St Michael is also trusted. Marks & Spencer's customers can now buy financial services carrying the Marks & Spencer guarantee of high quality and safety. But 'knickers don't mix well with investments' say the analysts. So would Marks & Spencer have been better to form an alliance and add a new brand for a different category?

The Virgin brand with Esso's financial muscle and Tesco's controls could mean an alliance made in heaven to a strategic alliance specialist. Such a dream team is already partly in place. Esso has an alliance with Tesco that involves trading from the same location, with Esso marketing the fuels and Tesco marketing and running the shop. The shop stocks certain Virgin brands. This is not a mega-deal but a simple sharing of day-to-day business issues of property and operational marketing.

Companies win in the marketplace by being different and original. Profitability comes from the perceived quality of the total offering. To avoid following the crowd, marketers in 'overcrowded' markets need to plan a differentiated approach and to target their products carefully. This chapter will explore the main reasons for some of the existing alliances of brands and describe a methodology for building successful co-branding alliances in the shop of the future.

History

Recent history contains many examples of retailers joining forces and co-branding. This is not to say that co-branding requires the intensity of a merger or takeover to join together two or more brands under 'one roof'. Because co-branding is an efficient way of increasing market opportunities quickly some obvious liaisons have been formed. Moreover, some were formed in order to find out the optimum process and then to copy it without maintaining the partnership.

Today's modern consumers are discerning and demand that their needs be met all of the time and at the right price. We live in a 24-hour society. Information about consumer shopping habits has never before been better and technology is improving all of the time to increase marketers' knowledge. The traditional retailers are facing consolidation in buying habits, and finding this tough. For example, consumers now find it easier to buy fresh meat from a food retailer on a Sunday than they did a decade ago from a traditional butcher. The market share of traditional retailers has been gobbled up by the ever quick-to-respond supermarket operators. They have built large out-of-town shopping parks and provided consumers with a one-stop shop. As the supermarkets have added more core skills to their businesses a mixture of governmental controls (i.e. restrictions in out-of-town developments) and market forces have created openings that have tested how far their brand's loyalty could be stretched. Tesco has used its brand strength to develop its business from food into areas that include pharmacy, banking, post offices, petrol, and many more. It is even rumoured that dentists and vets will be looking to set up their practices under the Tesco brand in the future. The superstores of the supermarket chains provide a perfect host environment for a plethora of co-branding opportunities. The success of Tesco and the other leading superstore groups has come from building their own label brands and stretching these brands into commodity categories that will shake off their outdated title of 'grocers' forever. But would consumers buy a car from them?

Recent research carried out by Irene Inskip at CLK, the London-based marketing consultancy, discovered that an amazing 20 per cent of respondents to their survey would buy a branded car from a supermarket and 15 per cent would buy an own label car (this rose to 20 per cent within the 35–45-year-old age group). The key issue for the supermarkets is whether or not they have the skills to serve these new markets profitably and for the long term. Can they do it on their own or do they need to bring in expertise by way of a co-brand partner?

Consumers trust the big brands of the food retailers. So managers of other brands will want to link with them to gain consumer trust by association for themselves.

In retailing everything has its place and everything had its time. Up until 1996 property developers would attract two conventional tenants, a department store and a supermarket, to be the anchor of any large out-of-town developments. Government restrictions made finding these tenants difficult. Middlebrook is a new development in Bolton. The 'anchor' tenant is Warner Bros Cinemas. The new Warner Bros Village multiplex is home for a number of integrated activities. The complex is open 24 hours a day and visitors, of whom there are 140,000 per week, can see a film, go out for a meal and do some shopping. A hotel has been built, as has a tennis complex. This centre has also attracted industry. Hitachi have built a 120-employee high-tech factory on the site and the Royal Bank of Scotland has established a call centre. The complex is a mini town. The centre makes a real difference to people's time-pressured lives. It is expected that 5000 people will live and work at Middlebrook; the centre has become a seedbed for co-branders.

Convenience stores have been around for some time. They have evolved as the locality support store. In 1927 the Southland Ice Company in America added the sale of watermelons to its ice business. They found that products stayed fresh if kept overnight packed in ice. Customers kept on asking for more things to be added and a retail store evolved. Today Southland Corporation is the owner of 7-Eleven, the largest brand of convenience stores in the world. In 1983 Southland bought Citgo, an oil company with outlets across the US. Petrol is a significant contributor to the sales and profits of convenience store operators. The sales of petroleum were an important draw for the consumer. While 7-Eleven had been marketing its own petroleum under its own brand, however, 7-Eleven petrol was not perceived by the consumers as a quality product, especially in comparison with Exxon and Texaco for example, so the 7-Eleven marketers set the price as the lowest on the street to draw customers into their stores. The effect was not good. Petrol customers were only interested in the cheap fuels and were not in the least interested in the high-priced quality branded goods in the stores. So 7-Eleven's sales were high in low-margin petrol and low in high-margin merchandise.

When the oil company Citgo was purchased, the Southland marketers kept the Citgo brand and co-branded with the 7-Eleven store. Consumers recognized the quality both on the forecourt and in the store. Then 7-Eleven co-branded with a number of other well-known brands like Mobil and Texaco and found that creating relationships with other co-branders was an excellent method to grow their store base and their profits for a smaller investment per store. The company has developed other co-brands apart from petrol; they include milk, dairy, fast food, soft drinks and ice.

In the UK, the oil companies control the real estate and are working to develop the skills and resources to upgrade their food offers. The food retailers want to be involved, they know how to do it but they don't have the sites. The oil companies' consumers demand more fresh products in the core offering of the forecourt stores. The oil companies have not developed their own distribution capability, preferring that their stores should be supplied by wholesalers and they therefore needed speedily to find a way of getting this difficult-to-control product range into their stores. The chosen route was to invite distributors and fresh food branding to be supplied by a specialist food retailer and buying into a franchise package.

In 1994, Q8 and Budgens formed a relationship that is based on such a franchise. The staff and stores belong to Q8 and, under a franchise and distribution agreement based on each location converted to the Budgens format, each receives Budgens' own label and proprietary products, together with pricing, promotional programmes and overall food retailing expertise.

This combining of skills has been successful. Most of the co-branders, in convenience- or forecourt-store retailing, that have conducted tests in the last three to four years have announced plans to develop more sites after completing successful tests. Consumers now see that these joint venture or 'JV' shops are better than other service station shops because they offer a better range of products, these products are of higher quality, prices are competitive, and value for money and customer service are both much improved.

Budgens is not necessarily perceived as being the equal of large brands like Tesco, Sainsbury and Safeway. But consumers using these smaller convenience stores on forecourts recognize the branding, associate Budgens with small stores and compare them favourably with the oil-industry shops and independent convenience store operators like Spar, Londis and Mace.

Brokers W. de Broe advised its corporate investors in September 1996 that this strategy was a good one. This is because of the risk of high investment costs of having to compete with the top food retailers in areas where there is evidence of market saturation. By creating new business in small stores Budgens neatly slipped the mantle of being a competitor of Tesco and gained support from its investors to exploit the opportunity of new store development.

Also well positioned to succeed in this alliance are Q8. Their relationship is not exclusively with Budgens and through being a franchisee they learnt many new ways of introducing new products and services through their large retail network. By benchmarking the results of these co-branded outlets further store growth can be achieved with or without Budgens.

When Sainsbury reacted to the market opportunity presented by home delivery they established a link with an unknown operator called Flanagans. This new market was developing fast and their relationship was one of the first co-branded developments in home deliveries. The relationship faltered and Sainsbury, armed with the experience of Flanagans, now run their own home delivery services. Somerfield acquired Flanagans for £2 million in March 1999. This is the other way of finding out how to do it.

Choosing a Partner

Merging two companies is like putting together two tribes: each has its own customs and culture. The people make the difference and any amalgamation can look good in principle, but if the chemistry is wrong everything will fail. Co-branding in retail is not a merger but two different cultures inevitably will be involved, even if they are part of the same parent company. In choosing the right partner in a retail operation the keys to success must be derived from the answers to the simple questions 'What's in it for me? What's in it for them?' If the answers to these questions can successfully be divined and reconciled, then success will result.

Picking the right location and the best store management are fundamental to retail success and play a large part in the selection of a co-brand. For example, an oil company often arranges for the companies' retail sites to be run by independent businessmen (i.e. licensees or franchisees). In working with Total in developing a co-branded forecourt and store, Alldays, who already had a large number of franchisees and licensees, identified the co-branding 'hinge' to be the entrepreneurial retail manager and a new franchise was formed. Total have made the investment and the relationship is cemented on Alldays producing consistent brand prosperity as a franchiser. Should the relationship fail, both parties stand to lose. Alldays will lose volume through their distribution system and the royalties on the merchandise sales and Total will have to develop a distribution system from scratch and invest in an expensive re-branding programme. The two companies, even though they operate with different cultures found a formula that links them in the lowest common denominator: the store and its manager.

In a different relationship similar principles have been adopted. Alldays and Victoria Wine teamed up in July 1998. Allied Domecq, the owner of Victoria Wine, has another brand that is already trading within most of Alldays' southern stores – Dunkin Donuts. The objective of the Victoria Wine link was to increase both companies' customer bases without huge investment in new shops. Their agreement allowed Victoria Wine to start selling a range of alcoholic drinks in Victoria Wine-branded display cases and fridges. The co-branding objectives of this joint venture look on the face of it to be a simple way of adding a new brand of store-within-a-store to an Alldays outlet.

This probably was a minor objective. For example, the tobacco companies have introduced gantries for the sale of tobacco in many thousands of stores, from multiples to independents, for many years. So the introduction of branded display cases and fridges is nothing new. On closer scrutiny there is much to be gained from this relationship for both parties.

Alldays and Total now operate 300 stores on forecourts. In the other stand-alone Alldays convenience stores alcohol is one of their main categories for sales and profits. Considerable pressure is being put on Government to allow the sale of alcohol from forecourt stores as licensing authorities all over the UK are rejecting the majority of applications from forecourt operators for the sale of alcohol. Should these restrictions be lifted, Alldays and Victoria Wine (who are the largest chain of off-licences in the UK) are well positioned to grow their businesses into forecourts. They have the expertise and track records of gaining licences all over the UK for their stand-alone or high-street stores. The two companies operating together create a valuable portfolio of relevant experience and responsibility. The authorities are more likely to trust them in new development applications. This version of co-branding will enable both parties to capitalize on a market opening gained from Government action.

Furthermore, the opportunity of supplying 300 off-licence shops within Alldays' joint venture with Total should be a significant business-builder for Victoria Wine. They will be able to rationalize their real-estate structure and exit from unprofitable sites in the vicinity of an Alldays store. This will have the effect of reducing their property exposure and maintaining their market share for a lesser investment into a retail outlet. Equally Alldays will benefit from Victoria Wine's consolidation of their retail estate by gaining first refusal as a preferred business partner on stores which they may consider disposing of. Victoria Wine keeps market share and Alldays expands theirs.

All parties have an equal amount to gain and lose from this relationship. To measure their risk is simple; what has the convenience store operator got apart from the Victoria Wine brand that will ensure that they, i.e. Alldays, will be focused on building the relationship and not just learning from them? The most likely answer is Dunkin Donuts. Should there be a falling out of the parties, Alldays stands to lose the Dunkin Donut brand from their other stores. So even though the scale of the Victoria Wine deal is at first small the opportunity of successful growth is high and failure would risk other profit areas. This co-branding relationship is therefore a strategic link-up between two large corporations with three brands and a huge collective property portfolio. They chose each other well.

Criteria for 'The Deal'

The joining of brands or combining of brands owned by a manufacturing culture with a retailer culture can build market share and prosperity for the parties involved. In choosing a partner the brand managers set up agreements from the lowest common denominator. Therefore common bonds are built through each tier of management and department of the companies involved. The main areas of commonality are as follows:

Property

Creating shops within shops or building shops on the same site is a well-tried and tested mechanic for successful co-branding. Retail locations get more expensive as more consumers walk or travel by. The better the property the more power its owners have to command which brands they want to co-brand with and under what circumstances they wish to deal. The properties need to fit.

Buying

Forming buying alliances enables greater volumes to be achieved from co-branders. In the above example of Alldays and Victoria Wine, the Allied Domecq brands sold through the rest of the Alldays chain probably benefited from distribution-cost savings on bulk purchases and created other avenues for profit gains and greater brand distribution.

Retail Operational Management

One store needs only one manager. Savings can be made from integrating two or more brands under the management of one person. This person can be an entrepreneurial franchisee or a company manager depending on the overall relationship. Co-branding is the sharing of management expertise not duplication.

Marketing, Advertising and Promotions

Joint promotions crossing the brand boundaries can allow for greater consumer benefit. In the US, Burger King heavily promotes Pillsbury products in its outlets and links are being created between the two companies that produce additional sales and profits for their owner Diageo. There has to be a complementary association.

Business Development

Working at the lowest level the management chain can bring its expertise to bear on business-building with only one party being responsible for the day-to-day operational management pressures. For example, an oil company's territory manager will be able to focus on the forecourt pricing structure within the store's competitive market area. This allows the convenience store operator to manage the day-to-day running of the retail outlet ensuring adequate staff training, stock management and overall customer service standards. The relationship is focused on maximizing what each party is best at. However, there are no reasons to co-brand if you can do it better yourself or create a new brand of your own as Shell did with its Select brand. It now has 900 Select Shops in its retail estate of 1858.

Decision-making Process

At the lowest level decisions can be taken to decide on the best locations from which the co-branding partnership is to be developed. It is unrealistic to assume that every store should be the ideal location to position the co-brands. Should this be the case the relationship would be better structured from the boardroom and entitled a merger. Management teams will make the difference as to whether the co-branding partnership is successful, there has to be compatibility.

What's in it for me and for them? What is my lowest common denominator? What is theirs? From whom will we have to gain authority to proceed? Who will manage the day-to-day issues? How much will each party be investing into the venture? What are the likely returns? These questions will have to be answered from conducting specific research. A detailed project brief should be prepared. The box overleaf shows a methodology that could be used in choosing the format and developing a co-branding partnership for a food retailer and an oil company:

Cross Benefits and Costs

In carrying out a complete analysis of the likely structure the cross benefits and costs will be clearly highlighted. A retailing co-branded relationship will enable both parties to share and save on investment and the costs of operating the stores. The relationship will almost always be built from the lowest common denominator, the store. The reduction of the property costs will be the first significant benefit.

Every retailer aspires to maximize his property utilization. Site selection, acquisition, construction, and fit-out and exterior branding demand high levels of investment. Should the convenience store or the oil company select not to co-brand, the average investment in a complete operation based on a forecourt will be considerable. For illustration purposes only this example puts the investment as £600,000. Table 4.1 shows how a convenience store operator and an oil company can benefit by co-branding and co-investing:

Brand managers carefully plan the price structures and promotional policy for their brands. In retail this falls to the category managers responsible for each category of the store's merchandise. Decision-makers pitch the levels of promotional activity and retail pricing according to a number of issues that includes an expectation of traffic flow. In a co-branding relationship the traffic flow can be altered according to the pricing structure. The oil industry is alone in the way that it sets the price of its fuels and publishes these prices on the roadside pole sign for all passing motorists to see, as price is one of the most important factors in consumers deciding to buy fuels. In the event of the co-branded oil company deliberately setting a higher than normal retail price the traffic on the forecourt will dramatically reduce and the convenience store operator will lose a substantial part of its market. A co-branded relationship needs to establish clear guidelines as to each party's market pricing and margin expectations. Pricing and promotional activity should be pitched at the normal

Table 4.1 Benefits of co-branding and co-investing

Investment levels into the site construction and fit-out	Convenience store operator	Oil company
Store Shelving, refrigeration, floors ceilings etc.	£250,000	Nil
Forecourt Pumps and underground storage, canopy and signage.	Nil	£250,000
Common areas Car park etc.	£50,000	£50,000
Total	£300,000	£300,000

PROJECT OBJECTIVE

To establish that the proposed joint venture with A Food Retailer and An Oil Company is the best alternative to maximize future sales and profits.

METHOD

1. Initial
- Sign confidential undertaking.
- Agree timetable / critical path.

2. Analysis
- Is there an existing agreement?
- Identify both brand strengths and weaknesses.
- Compare consumer groups for compatibility.
- Identify differences in existing trading terms of common suppliers.
- Identify sources and compatibility of data from existing operations.
- Identify additional costs or likely benefits.
- Review distribution and management systems.
- Identify key project personnel.

All known information has been collated.

3. Market assessment
- Identify retail pricing strategies for both brands.
- Compare the current sales mix.
- Identify any additional operational requirements.
- Establish distribution costs to a co-branded outlet.
- Confirm point of difference and compare to competitors.
- Identify industry margin achievements.
- Establish the new margins.
- Does the co-branded relationship enhance the achievement of the whole Networks' objectives?
- Conclusions.

Agree this is the situation

4. Appraisal process
- Agree period of analysis for test locations.
- Identify test locations.
- Conduct a demographic profile of both brands' test stores.
- Identify proposition / point of difference.
- Appraise the following:
  - Consumer perception;
  - Sales & profits by product category (including promotions);
  - Own label participation;
  - Likely growth rate projections;

▶

– Range, pricing and promotional policy (Shop and Fuel);
– Distribution service;
– Shop trading hours;
– Store operations i.e. shrinkage, labour;
– Stock-holding.
- Define optimum agreement type i.e. Franchise, license, Joint development agreement (JDA), trading or distribution.

5. Strategic review and recommendations
- Complete a SWOT analysis for each test site.
- Review objectives.
- Presentation of alternatives.
- Development potential for the joint networks.

Conclude objectives, agree strategy and implementation programme

levels for the existing trading locations. Apart from the likely de-railing of the relationship, combative pricing will confuse the consumer too.

A convenience store contains many co-branding opportunities and alternatives. A typical location could contain a number of different brands. Cross benefits can be achieved by linking promotional offers of the co-branders in a multiplex' type outlet.

These locations could contain the following: Esso's petrol linked to Tesco Express convenience stores, automatic telling machines from The Royal Bank of Scotland, Burger King and Domino Pizza food centres, Victoria Wine's range of alcohol with Blockbuster Video, a Post Office and a Camelot lottery installation. Each brand could reward its customer's loyalty with an offer on one of the other co-brander's products or services. This is branding 'convenience'.

A multiplex property development would have a similar emphasis. At the Middlebrook complex in Bolton, referred to earlier, the developer attracted the tenants using the cinema as the anchor tenant. Potential occupiers could decide whether they wanted to take part on this basis. The cinema, central theme of

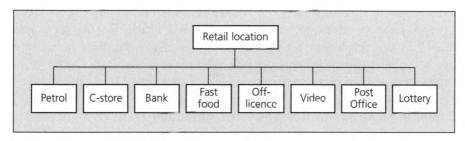

Figure 4.1 A 'multiplex' type of retail outlet

the location, was attractive to leisure-seekers and this theme set the pace for the brands that would profit from the profile of the customer groups visiting the site. The essential difference of this type of location from the forecourt convenience store is that a number of brands will be competing to take part, and the site owner is not a retailer but a developer. This neighbourly version of co-branding allows for promotional activity to be created by the occupiers to strengthen the appeal of the whole site. For example, for the family visit to the cinema the ticket purchase could trigger a link to a special offer fast food meal followed by a discounted swim in the leisure centre's pool or vice versa.

Co-branding agreements, in comparison with mergers or amalgamations, can rarely split the profit share equally. It is quite usual for both parties to make the same returns as their other operations but not the same as each other. The agreements should not prohibit the sales or profitable growth of either party unless it is as a direct result of unfair play involving the other (for example pricing). The benefit of a co-branded relationship comes from enhancing the normal returns on sales and capital through a reduced investment and cost base. All parties benefit from the collective branding of one location and each prospers in the way he knows best.

Workable Structures

The most workable structures of retailer co-branding are the Joint Development Agreement and the Franchise. Franchising provides a large choice of brands for independent entrepreneurs who run their own businesses or corporations, to add many additional brands to their strength in management. Franchising has given brand owners the opportunity for new development utilizing franchisee capital to fund the growth. Joint development agreements are best for large organizations where a number of retail locations under their direct control can be utilized. The two lowest common denominators are: a) JDA – retail locations, b) franchising – store management.

When two or more retail brands partner, their properties become the backbone to the best structure. A company with a large number of prime properties is more likely to choose well-known brands and invite their managers to tender to join them in these properties. Yet two growing companies that may have large numbers of properties in existence, or planned in the near future, are going to want to share the development costs or 'mirror image' each other's growth ambitions.

Example 1 – the Joint Development Agreement

Let us assume that the senior management of both a food retailer and an oil company have agreed to co-brand and to develop jointly on each other's locations. Their agreement anticipates the development of 100 stores. Each to provide 50 'host locations'.

The food retailer already has a number of 'own-branded' fuel operations on its superstore car parks and currently gets supply of motor fuels from the 'spot market' where it has experienced difficulties in supply and quality. The company has just developed a new convenience-store concept and is keen to roll out an aggressive expansion programme but has been thwarted by a lack of suitable sites. It has built a new distribution system to deliver to its new small stores and is keen to gain volume in order to justify its investment.

The oil company has developed a new convenience-store format based on consultation with its consumers. They have consistently asked for fresher products and more convenience foods to be added to their shop ranges. Their retailers are predominantly independent business people. They own at the minimum the stock in their stores and nearly a third of the oil company's branded locations are 'dealers' where the individual owns the whole site and trades with the oil company by way of a supply agreement for fuels and shop branding and design. The oil company wants to develop this new shop format on only a small proportion of their sites. The purchasing team does not have the power to insist that their retailers stock the range or sell out at the same retail prices. They need to find an alternative method of distribution that is the only source for a particular branded fresh food range. Their consumers are confused and the brand manager is calling for consistency of offer.

Both companies take action and search the marketplace for suitable co-branders. The analysts identify a number of alternatives and an initial agreement is reached to establish a test on a limited amount of stores. Each partner being satisfied that there are enough suitable locations available for development.

Their 'heads of agreement' could look like the illustration in the box on the following page. This agreement keeps the investment, the costs and the benefits split into each company's domain of expertise. Each company gets 50 new stores to trade from at half the cost of doing it themselves. They have only had to invest in their operations and in the case where they are the owners or the host store they are only responsible for the investment into the common areas. The food company's vertically integrated support systems and range eradicate the supply and in-store marketing issues faced by the oil company. Should the agreement and resultant programme be a success then both companies can review their commitment to a further programme, or utilize the agreement format and progress with another partner.

In a rising market where both companies are acquisitive this agreement can be made with a number of different brands or companies. If one of the party's markets is consolidating then the trust in this agreement has to be absolute.

JOINT DEVELOPMENT AGREEMENT

The agreement anticipates joint development of properties owned by both parties, with the following 'mirror image' terms applicable to all transactions irrespective of ownership.

LEASE

Valuation: Owner establishes fair market value of land; value subject to mutual agreement (or appraisal upon failure to agree).

Term: 5 years with further 3-year options.

Rent and other charges: tenant pays X per cent constant annual rent based on 50 per cent of the fair market value of land (fixed flat rent for the entire term). Uniform business rates, common area maintenance and common utilities split 50:50.

The per cent constant rate is negotiated annually; any renegotiated rate is applicable to new sites only.

Construction: Retailer constructs and pays for its store. Oil company constructs and pays for the motor fuels facility (including all the fuels equipment). The owner constructs and pays for the common area improvements.

Maintenance: Each party maintains its respective improvements and equipment. Owner maintains common area (but is reimbursed on a 50:50 basis).

Early termination: lessee has option to terminate on third anniversary upon six months notice.

MOTOR FUELS AGREEMENT

Commission: Oil company pays Retailer X pence per litre sold.

Agreement allows for annual renegotiations of the commission rate; any renegotiated commission will be applied to all joint development locations (old and new).

Inventory and pricing: Oil company retains the title to all motor fuels and sets the retail prices of the fuels. The retailer retains title to all merchandise sales within the store and sets the retail prices of the store merchandise.

Credit cards: Retailer accepts the oil company and other approved cards for payment of merchandise and motor fuel sales. No charge to retailer for motor fuel sales on any card; retailer pays market discount rate on merchandise sales on all cards.

Environment controls: Oil company's responsibility.

Other products: Retailer will sell the oil company's premium motor oils and other lubricants and transmission fluid exclusively in the retailer's store. The oil company agrees not to sell or promote any products competitive with the retailer.

Example 2 – the Franchise Agreement

The second example is more common – the franchise agreement or in certain cases a management contract. The franchise example is as follows. The food retailer has developed a café-type restaurant in most of its superstores. The restaurant serves traditional fare from hot meals through to cold snacks. Analysis of the loyalty scheme it launched three years ago identified that there are new categories of consumer groups using the store for their shopping and leisure activities. But only one of these groups is utilizing the services of the café so management wants to introduce a 'food court' into the store where it can sell a variety of fast food offers, from fish 'n' chips to burgers and pizzas, to suit all groups. The main fast food brands have all developed a shop-within-a-shop concept and airports and mainline railway stations throughout the UK contain good examples of food courts and other co-branders. The food retailer invites a number of fast food operators to compete for a franchise agreement to be co-branders within their superstores.

The food retailer is making the investment and is therefore taking the main risk. By involving different franchised brands the control of the development remains with them. The quota of new store developments can be agreed at the outset depending on the fast food company's brand or market strength. The food retailer has the customer flow and is in a position to create a market and jostle the alternatives in ensuring the best deals. The food retailer also keeps his options open to move fast if there is a change in market conditions or an adverse consumer reaction to one or more of the brands. The agreement could also be based on a license agreement where exclusively one party in a territory manages the brand. The main headings above would mostly remain the same.

Some companies sell concessions to trade within a host environment. The food retailer (or department store) would have become the landlord and most likely received rentals either fixed or a rent linked to turnover (or a mixture of both) from the in-store developments set by the location. In this example the concessionaire company would have had all the investment risk. Arcadia, the former Burton clothing group, claims one of its main sources of income comes from rental revenues from its concessions granted to other brands from within its stores.

Does Size Matter?

Co-branding brings many advantages to those companies who do not have the necessary expertise or the scale. In UK convenience retailing the financial muscle of the oil company dwarfs that of the convenience store operator. They

FRANCHISE AGREEMENT

Franchise agreement between a food retailer and a fast food retailer. This agreement would anticipate the development of a number of restaurants within the food retailer's supermarkets during a fixed period of time.

LEASE

Term: Fast food company will grant a 5-year franchise term with a further 5-year option to food retailer. Food retailer will provide fast food company with up to X host trading locations for the franchise term.

Early termination: Food retailer has the option to terminate the franchise agreement within X months of the start of the agreement should the sales performance be less than 50 per cent of forecast.

Rent and other charges: Food retailer will pay all annual rents, uniform business rates, common area maintenance and common utilities.

Construction: Food retailer will construct and pay for the fast food company food facility. Food retailer also constructs and pays for the common area improvements. Fast food company will specify all foodservice equipment that will be purchased by food retailer. Fast food company will assist in the management of the restaurant layout and design.

Maintenance: Food retailer will maintain the common areas and the restaurant. Food retailer will introduce improvements to the restaurant and equipment as specified by fast food company from time to time.

OPERATING AGREEMENT

Franchise fee: Food retailer will pay fast food company £X (plus VAT) per restaurant to cover the following:
- Professional fees including:
- Kitchen layout and interior design (but excluding architects costs);
- Legal and consultancy costs;
- Artwork supplied for trademarks and logos;
- Staff and management training with a minimum of 2 weeks' senior management time, with follow-up visits twice per week for the first month of trading, thereafter the standard operations audit per month with more visits as required.

Royalty: Food retailer will pay fast food company x per cent of gross turnover on all foodservice items sold.

Advertising: Food retailer will pay fast food company an initial advertising fee of £X (plus VAT) to cover local advertising and a monthly fee of x per cent of gross turnover.

Inventory and pricing: Food retailer retains the title to the foodservice inventory and fast food company will recommend and agree the foodservice retail prices with food retailer.

▶

> **Credit cards:** All approved credit cards by food retailer will be accepted for purchases of foodservice items. All credit card charges will be the responsibility of food retailer. Payment for foodservice items will be undertaken only through the fast food company cash registers.
>
> **Environment and Quality controls:** Health and Safety and compliance with the various Acts governing the sale of food will be the responsibility of food retailer. Fast food company will supply an operations and training system to assist in this compliance. A quality assurance programme will also be put in place and maintained by fast food company.
>
> **Standards:** Failure to achieve recognized standards as specified in the operations manual could result in the termination of the franchise agreement by fast food company.
>
> **Other products:** Only fast food company products will be sold in the restaurant. Food retailer agrees not to sell or promote any foodservice products in the same store which are competitive with those of the fast food company range in force at the time of opening.

do, however, need each other. Fuel-based convenience stores need oil company expertise. As a partner they should provide fuels marketing skill and know-how, the property supply line and investment expertise.

The food retailers need more sites because building more superstores has been made difficult through the Government's restrictions on new out-of-town developments. Food retailers captured a large proportion of the petroleum market and caused a bitter price war that lasted two years. The biggest defensive attack on them came from Esso's Pricewatch promotion; that has now ended. The full retail proposition on each site now holds the key to future success. This means that in future the oil companies' growth will have to come from investment in the fuels selling process, while non-fuels growth is likely to be achieved by finding a retail partner who will invest in retailing and its support structure. The food retailers therefore will have to learn how to operate convenience stores; perhaps they will choose to learn from a co-branding partnership with a worldwide brand of the stature of 7-Eleven.

Should the industry be concerned about the co-branding partnerships of the largest companies like the Esso–Tesco alliance that was announced in 1998? Esso manufactures and sells petrol; Tesco is a retailer and sells petrol on its 275 forecourts. Tesco gets 100 stores from Esso for food store development. If this is the proposed alliance structure then it is just sensible business practice. The pressure is on Esso to find and make the right sites available to Tesco. Store locations and hypermarket volumes appear to be the levers that will keep these two in check and others who will surely follow.

Conclusion

All day and night they come. Mostly working people moving to and from their jobs. In the early morning there are many from the offices and factories. Before midday the traffic increases. In mid afternoon the kids begin to arrive. Late afternoon and evening brings the tide of returning workers, stopping to buy vital things that have accumulated during the day. Many essentials are ready to be found, purchased and carried to homes. During the night until dawn they still come looking for the comfort displayed by the lights. As the sun comes up and another 24-hour cycle begins, the process will repeat itself. People's lives will be touched, their needs will be served.

The customer relies on us; we rely on them. It is up to us to be ready for them whenever they want us. A co-branding partnership that does not put the customer first will not succeed and nor does it deserve to. Look after the customer and the customer will look after you. Co-branders build on their own strengths and react to changing market conditions. They are alive to being copied by a partner and have got the customer in their focus. Equal partners have joint development agreements, non-equal partners live within a franchise agreement and the rest are space concessions. Co-branders improve customer choice, quality of service and profitability.

SWOT analysis of co-branding for retail

Strengths

- Ability to adapt to changing markets.
- Fast companies able to make fast decisions can benefit from working with like-minded organizations.
- Building of two in-house brands (Shell fuels, Select shops).
- Uniform marketing and promotions.
- Provide one service in exchange for another.
- Retail property growth.
- Benefit by association.

Weaknesses

Disguises unexciting results.
Recession protection.
Long-term association with poor performer or weak brand.
Dropping of standards because of the inability of poor franchisees.
Customer or governmental intervention.

Opportunities

Industry restructuring link with the new leaders.
Outsource to experts.
Introduce a culture change through a new organization.
Learn a new trade.
Improve consumer trust.
Extend offer and evolve more services.
Increase market penetration.
Improve quality and profitability.
Commitment made to new ideas.
Joint promotional activity.
Increased intelligence of shared consumer shopping habits.

Threats

Changing consumer.
Government legislation i.e. out-of-town development restrictions.
New entrants from overseas or different market sectors.
Consumer confusion.
Safety scares and product recalls.

5 | Ingredient Branding

Marc Smit

Introduction

Ingredient branding is a specific category of co-branding. Whilst co-brands bring together brands in a single offer to the consumer, ingredient brands differ in that they are a component of the end product. This chapter will look at what lies behind this generic and often misused name in an attempt to establish what ingredient branding is. We will then investigate what has to be taken into account when moving into ingredient branding (the why?) and the optimal brand strategy to do so (the how?).

Defining Ingredient Branding

To secure market channels in a fast-changing economy, brands can play a key role in establishing a company or product in the consumer's mind. Intel has been highly successful at managing the value chain without integrating vertically. To keep up, companies are investing heavily in intellectual capital (management, R&D, etc.). The sums involved create strong barriers to entry to some industries – for example IT and pharmaceuticals. Exploiting these investments has become a competitive weapon and an important strategic issue. Either vertically integrated or vertically specialized, some companies have decided to exploit their technologies indirectly, in original equipment manufacturer relationships. To leverage corporate reputation and technological excellence, a smaller number of these companies are communicating – branding - this presence. This is what we mean by 'ingredient branding'.

Ingredient branding is a strategic tool to leverage the company's excellence. By jumping further downstream, it allows a direct relationship with the customer to be built. By building awareness and, it is hoped, loyalty, this strategy, providing it is coherent and long-term, can shift the balance of power in the value chain. Thus value generation potential is shifting towards the supplier of ingredient brands through a demand 'pull effect' (Please refer to Jan Lindemann, Chapter 7 for further information on brand valuation).

The financial advantages are clear. Not only does it enable exploitation of R&D investments, it also makes it possible to focus on core competencies, to secure time to market and demand for further technological developments, to lower commercialization costs and to benefit from complementary intangible and tangible assets[1] (crucial to go to market). The inherent risk can, however, be high – especially in terms of brand equity for the supplying company.

Categorizing Ingredient Branding

As we said in the introduction, ingredient branding has a number of underlying strategic benefits. They differ from one company to another, from one business model to another. They can be:

- Branding the invisible and creating a demand 'pull effect';
- Setting up an umbrella to exploit innovation and faster speed to market;
- Leveraging R&D investments and managing the product life-cycle;
- Exploiting value chain strategy;
- Leveraging of your brand's core values, credibility (diffusion of reputation) and superior product perceived and actual qualities.

Ingredient brands should build a pact between the company and its customers. Like most intangibles, intellectual property can be leveraged in direct or indirect exploitation. According to Parr and Sullivan (1966) direct exploitation will be likely to happen when:

- The intellectual property is in the main line of the company's business;
- The business has all the necessary resources to fully exploit the intellectual property;
- There might be too much liability in realizing the exploitation to others;
- The intellectual property might be retained for use as a trading card in other infringement litigation;
- Intellectual property might potentially be too difficult to control in the hands of others;
- The intellectual property is untransferrable;
- Potential royalties may be too low to warrant the costs and/or risks of transfer.

If the company decides to exploit the intellectual property indirectly, it will do

so by transferring an asset in exchange for a financial reward. This exchange
can take various forms, various risk and return patterns:

- Outright sale.
- Licensing and cross-licensing.
- Extensions.
- Joint venture.
- Franchising.

Indirect exploitation is a way to maximize R&D investments. Coupled with
state-of-the-art branding it is also a way to develop a franchise that will pave
the way for further innovation.

Famous Ingredient Brands

There is a 'pool' of famous ingredient brands. Intel, Gore-Tex, Lycra, Teflon,
Trinitron, DigitalDNA, Dolby, NutraSweet, AirMax, are all ingredients that
have achieved superior levels of awareness. Despite the fact that they stem from
different business models, these ingredient brands are too often seen as a
somewhat undifferentiated pool. For the purpose of clarity, we will split them
into three main categories: 'supplier' ingredient brands; 'manufacturer to
supplier' ingredient brands; and 'proprietary' ingredient brands.

Supplier ingredient brands

Focusing their competencies on supplying quality technologies, these
companies (Dolby and Intel for example) are vertically specialized. They have
often managed to shift the value generating power in the value chain by
communicating their USP directly to the consumer. The key success factors are:

- Consistency and long-term commitment.
- Co-operation with chosen original equiment manufacturers (OEMs).
- Constant investment in building the brand.

Compared to other undifferentiated suppliers of components, they have
managed to secure higher loyalty and increased market share by creating
demand and thereby adding value to the entire chain.

Manufacturer to Supplier Ingredient Brands

In contrast to the previous category, these companies (Motorola with
DigitalDNA and Monsanto with NutraSweet for example) are present at

different stages of the value chain (fully or partially vertically integrated) and find themselves in situations where they are both supplying and manufacturing, sometimes across different business areas. They exploit their technologies directly as well as indirectly and sometimes operate over a wide array of business areas. Given the overlaps, the ingredient brand strategy will hence be much more complex and risky.

Proprietary Ingredient Brands

Either developed in-house or acquired (exclusively or not), this last category, which includes exclusive brands like Nike's AirMax and DriFit, does not strictly belong to the general ingredient branding category. Branded in their own corporate environment, these technologies are not exploited in other environments and usually have a confined role of product differentiator or brand attribute.

However, it is crucial to understand and include them since they are often associated with ingredient brands (despite clear differences in the business model). They are often perceived by customers as undifferentiated from any of the ingredient brands of the above mentioned categories, creating consumer confusion.

Case Studies

Supplier Ingredient Brands

In this category we find among others:

- Dolby.
- Intel.
- Gore-Tex.
- Cisco.

These brands have common origins in supplying technologies. Starting with a narrowly focused value proposal, they have all seized the monolithic – the single, all-embracing – brand route. In order to leverage their brand and the superior qualities of their technology, they have invested heavily to establish their name. Given the limited stretch and the obvious value proposal, a monolithic brand is clearly a powerful strategy.

Intel is a vivid illustration of this. After years of using generic code numbers (the 86 generation), Intel Inc. decided, in the beginning of the 80s, to change its strategy. The ultimate way to keep (and protect) its leading role in the supply of chips was to develop a brand that would convey the idea of superior quality and reliability. The first move was made by launching the 'Red X' campaign. A red X was brushed on the Intel logo. This campaign was not particularly successful and, soon after its launch, was replaced by the now famous Intel Inside campaign. Over the last decade, Intel Inc. has not ceased to grow. Only 10–20 per cent of advertising investments are spent yearly on the Intel Inside advertisements with a much larger share going to joint advertising with the companies bearing the Intel Inside mark. To take part in an OEM relationship with Intel, companies have to contribute to the advertising stream in co-operation with Intel. Along with Microsoft, Intel is now in a dominant position in the so-called WINTEL platform. At a time when PCs are increasingly falling into the commodity category, Intel has managed to build sustainable differentiation. The Intel Inside presence has become a key purchase criterion. In a way, this case magnifies the virtues of branding. Intel Inc. has remained in vertical specialization and, despite its total lack of control in the value chain downstream, Intel Inc. has managed to reverse the power towards the supplier. The high level of awareness and trust built in customers' perceptions has definitely had a 'pull effect'. Intel will create the demand' (A. Grove, CEO of Intel).*

Gore-Tex Inc. did not hesitate so much before clearly backing the Gore-Tex mark. Today, Gore-Tex Inc. is introducing new fibres and treatments with distinct features. To avoid customer confusion, Gore-Tex Inc. has also decided to introduce new brands, strongly endorsed by the Gore-Tex 'umbrella'. The main rationale behind this move is that Gore-Tex Inc. is to establish a portfolio of technologies that have different characteristics. The Gore-Tex brand becomes an umbrella, instilling trust and confidence in the customers' mind. Activent by Gore-Tex and Windstopper by Gore-Tex are two of these new brands. Research undertaken by Interbrand (pan-European qualitative focus groups) clearly shows that Gore-Tex is strongly associated with breath-ability and warmth. It is perceived as being a technology suited for extreme conditions and cold weather, but slightly unfashionable. In order to leverage the brand and its quality values, developing endorsed identities like Activent by Gore-Tex and Windstopper by Gore-Tex will allow Gore-Tex to develop a new value proposal and position them according to their specificities.

Cisco Systems, a leading supplier of Internet and data networking equipment for many years, has recently expanded its branding strategy beyond that associated with its company brand and logo. There are several new logos for different uses, but each prominently features the 'Cisco' name, along with

---

* For a more detailed examination of Intel's marketing strategy see Tim Jackson, 'Intel: the Inside Story' in *Market Leader*, Winter 1998, 38–42.

distinguishing graphics and text. The Cisco Powered Network programme (already referred to in Chapter 2) and the Cisco NetWorks programme are the two major new initiatives.

For certain product areas, such as digital set-top boxes for use with television sets, Cisco is licensing certain of its software and technologies to specialist companies manufacturing these products. As Cisco explains:

> The Cisco NetWorks Product Branding Program enables authorized product development partners to use a special Cisco logo on their products and in their advertising and promotional materials. This logo tells their customers that the Cisco NetWorks-branded products deliver reliable network connectivity and interoperability, enabled by software technologies from Cisco Systems, the company recognized by many as a world-class leader in networking for the Internet. ... That increased confidence and recognition gives you an extra advantage as you expand into new markets and new channels of distribution.

By setting the criteria for participation in the program, Cisco ensures that authorized product development partners produce network-ready products that can truly deliver reliable network connectivity and interoperability. Cisco also underlined the competitive advantage the company would get, namely to accelerate time-to-market for new classes of network devices'.[2]

By specializing in the earliest stage of the value chain, suppliers of technologies have to shape the customers' perception and attempt to 'control' the purchase decision in their favour. This strategy requires heavy advertising investments and constant product innovation. Being first in consumers' minds is not only a definite advantage but also creates a high barrier to new market entries. To sustain this competitive advantage, these companies have usually established an umbrella that allows for technological improvement and growth.

Manufacturer to Supplier Ingredient Brands

In this category we find:

- Motorola and DigitalDNA.
- Monsanto and NutraSweet.
- DuPont de Nemours and Lycra, Teflon, etc.[3]
- Akzo Nobel and Sympatex.
- Lucasfilm and THX.

All the above mentioned companies share similar characteristics: a multiproduct portfolio and are active both in supplying technologies and in manufacturing and servicing.

DuPont de Nemours is probably the best regarded ingredient brand company. Through a very powerful and clear strategy it has managed to establish standalone brands – endorsed to a greater or lesser extent by the corporate brand. This strategy has allowed the company to move into many different technological fields and reach top-of-mind awareness with consumers:

- More than 98 per cent of consumers know the DuPont name and reputation.
- Two out of three consumers view DuPont as a supplier of high-quality products.
- Eight out of ten consumers are more likely to buy a product when they see the DuPont name.
- The DuPont name positively impacts awareness, believability of product claims and purchase likelihood.
- Associating the DuPont name with new and less known brands increases the purchase interest and believability by 10 per cent.[4]

DuPont's involvement in the clothing field is strong, through its fibres' division. In a recent study by Interbrand, we investigated the buying process in sports clothing. It is interesting to see how fibre technologies are ranked relatively low in people's conscious buying criteria in order of importance. The criteria were:

- Comfort and fit.
- Quality.
- Price.
- Style.
- Colour.
- Brand (Fibre technology).
- Durability.

According to our research, most clothing technologies only help to strengthen the post-purchase confirmation. The merits of the technology will increase the level of confidence in purchasing the garment, only after the other criteria have been fulfilled. However, subconsciously, consumers acknowledge the impact of brand as a vector of quality. Brand, technology and quality are overlapping concepts rendering it difficult to classify buying criteria clearly. It was nevertheless obvious that there are only a few technologies that have built their reputation up to a level where they can impact consumers' choice alongside the product brand. Lycra and Gore-Tex have unquestionably gained this position.

Motorola has also launched an ingredient brand strategy with DigitalDNA. As in the cases we have already discussed, Motorola went for an endorsed identity (DigitalDNA by Motorola). But in high-tech fields, such strategies are highly complex: consumers are increasingly confused by bewildering choices. The boundaries between product, corporate brand, service and technology are often unclear. The fast pace of change and constant need to adapt the offer frequently creates confusing brand architectures.

In March 1999, IBM unveiled a plan to exploit its technologies in other brands' hardware. By agreeing on a cross-selling technology platform, Dell will use IBM's technologies in a number of applications. Dell has always been one of IBM's largest buyers of technologies and this move has formalized and secured the existing relationship between the two companies. According to a Dell spokesman, 'most important for Dell is to always have the latest technologies and to market them first'. With the new deal, Dell will benefit from the innovation without having to commit to in-house R&D investments. 'Straight after its $16 billion pact with Dell, IBM is forming a $3 billion alliance in parts and technology with EMC, a rival in the business of making data-storage systems. IBM announced a loss of $992m in 1998 on its PC business.' (*The Economist*, 20 March 1999.) Clearly no company can afford to sustain for long such losses, and these moves support IBM's strategic vision to focus on software, services and technological products. According to J.T. Vanderslice, Vice President of the IBM Technology Group, 'IBM increases the size of its commercial opportunities as well as its distribution channels ... our approach to the marketplace is to take our technologies through IBM channels and non-IBM channels.' If IBM were to brand this presence, they would have to be very careful to define the boundaries between its core and the periphery clearly as well as its role in the value chain. Moving away from PC assembly and focusing on innovation and services, is a strategic decision to move towards future growth.

NutraSweet is a stand-alone brand that has, without any endorsement, been a success story since its launch. Owned by Monsanto, NutraSweet has played a key role in the diet trend. The brand conveys such powerful values of quality and trust in consumers' minds that it has become a crucial consumer product in its own right. Nutrasweet, for example, wanted to bolster its image, so it encouraged and co-financed advertising campaigns by its clients' brands. In turn, these clients' brands endorsed Nutrasweet and endowed it with connotation of pleasure and affective values, until now sugar's exclusive domain.' (J.N. Kapferer, *Strategic Management*, London, September 1997, p. 87.)

The major challenge for companies that have an established reputation in manufacturing and servicing is to protect themselves from the risks inherent to OEM situations. Sharing their intellectual capital with competing companies entails obvious threats. On top of product quality issues, which the company does not directly control, the corporate brand and its reputation are at stake.

Using an endorsed brand strategy, to whatever extent, allows the company to convey trust without committing to the full guarantee that it promises on its own products and services. The focus on core competencies and the need to concentrate on value creation forces a company to develop partnerships and co-operate. The investment in R&D has to be leveraged, and it is often more profitable to create loyalty and security of earnings in OEM environment than to commit to vertical integration. With such complexity the brand strategy then becomes crucial to glue all the constituent parts together.

Proprietary Ingredient Brands

In this case, the dynamics are completely different. Proprietary ingredient brands are technologies that are exclusively exploited in their owner's controlled brand environment. These technologies are either developed in-house or bought with exclusive rights.

In this category we find among others:

- AirMax by Nike.
- DriFit by Nike.
- DMX by Reebok.
- Trinitron by Sony.
- CDI by Mitsubishi.

By branding these technologies, manufacturers can build brand equity in protected environments. These technologies often add or reinforce an existing attribute (e.g. performance and innovation for Nike), introduce a new idea within the brand or differentiate their products.

Having a controlled and clear environment eases the process of establishing the technology. Moreover, the investments needed are far less than for the categories of ingredient brand listed above. Usually, these technologies are an integral part of the product offering, not requiring a unique stream of advertising. With the clear advantage of control, proprietary ingredient brands do, however, have a major pitfall. They lack the 'moment of truth' of establishing themselves over the years by their intrinsic qualities and advertising dollars – as Gore-Tex did. In many cases, consumers have the impression of being sold a recycled version of an existing technology. The overall brand strength as well as the brand architecture is crucial in establishing a proprietary technology where technological credibility is key to the purchase decision.

A look at sports brands is helpful to understand the specifics of this category. Nike has been very successful in using branding to position proprietary technologies. Nike has established technologies over time with very straight-forward value proposals. In shoes, the evolution of technology went from

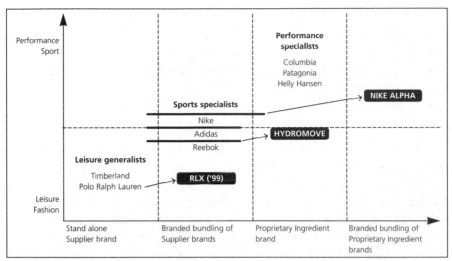

Figure 5.2 Strategies for establishing technological credibility
Source: Interbrand

AirMax to AirZoom and TunedAir. The idea of 'Air' was established as an umbrella, whilst the second component of the name precisely defined the nature of the Air (cushioning or stability). In apparel, we see a similar strategy with Nike 'Fit' (DriFit, StormFit, ClimaFit, and ThermaFit). This flexible and benefit-driven approach is a clever shortcut to establish technologies over time, under a clear and easy-to-understand umbrella. This strategy acknowledges the specificity of proprietary ingredient branding; it should be consumer-oriented and easy to understand.

Reebok, on the other hand, has followed a different strategy by attempting to convey technological credibility through its naming strategy: DMX and Hexalite (for shoes) and Hydromove (for apparel). Less straightforward in terms of benefit, some of these technologies are used as a platform for upgrades (DMX6, DMX8, DMX10 as well as Hydromove and Hydromove Plus). The use of X seems to be a recurrent tactic to name technologies. It is interesting to note that Polo (Ralph Lauren) will launch its own umbrella for technologies (bundling of Gore-Tex) under the RLX name. As mentioned above, proprietary technologies largely depend on the overall brand strength to generate credibility and are often used as vehicles to increase it.

In 1999, Nike went a step further in branding its technologies by launching Alpha. The stated intent is that Alpha is not:

- A sub-brand.
- A collection.
- A technology.
- A gadget/a marketing bomb.
- For the elite.

Alpha is:

- For athletes.
- A promise to create the best peforming products.
- A specific answer to the needs of sportsmen, by category of sport.
- A long-term commitment.
- A concept comprising apparel, shoes and accessories.
- A high-performance label.[5]

Along the lines of Nike's evolution, this move is designed to simplify even further consumers' choice. Alpha is a standard of quality that stretches across the product line and has been designed to identify the best of Nike. Aside from features and benefits, Alpha is much rather a philosophy. This will most probably alter the boundary between order winners and qualifiers, and raise the branding bar in the sports industry even higher. However, is the consumer ready and educated enough (especially in Europe) to understand the value proposal?

Trinitron by Sony is another good example. Despite its presence in OEM environments, the Trinitron brand is only featured on Sony televisions. It has been positioned as a guarantee of superior product quality. By deciding not to share the trademark, Sony is clearly drawing a line between its products and those from the competition. The strategy is to confer differentiation on its own products whilst at the same time exploiting its technology. CDI, by Mitsubishi, is another example where proprietary protected technology has been used to revamp the brand – with strong advertising investment. Their proprietary injection technology is used to leverage the company's innovation capability and instil a more technological idea to the brand.

Differing from the other categories, proprietary ingredient brands have a much more discrete role to play: adding or reinforcing an attribute; introducing a new idea to the brand, or strengthening overall product differentiation. The brand-building efforts are often part of the company's corporate–product branding. This close intimacy with the parent brand allows for more freedom. At the same time, however, the launch of the technology and its success will be strongly reliant on the brand's technological credibility.

Parameters

From our experience and the above mentioned case studies, we can now draw some tentative conclusions concerning the branding issues faced by companies that are planning to brand their OEM ingredient technology. There are a number of parameters that will have to be investigated in order to determine the brand strategy to be followed. Let us consider the 'whys' and the 'hows'.

Strategic Decision (why?)

What are the factors that have to be taken into account before a company decides to bring branding to its OEM relationships? If these can be determined then this will allow us to judge whether or not the company should use ingredient branding, and the best approach it should follow.

Value

Will ingredient branding add more value than a non-branding OEM relationship? Will the investment in branding add value to the innovation process by improving time to market and creating demand?

Can the company invest in establishing a brand? The investment required to establish an ingredient brand is considerable and requires a long-term commitment.

Could this technology be a key value driver for the consumer? As said earlier on, ingredient branding is a technique which allows a strategy to be built with the consumer whilst reversing the power balance within the value chain. In order to create a demand 'pull effect', the ingredient has to be meaningful (or has to be able to develop perceived meaning) to the consumer.

Can you convince OEM partners to co-operate? Without the OEM partner's strategic co-operation, there will be no ingredient branding. Depending on the power structure within the value chain as well as the degree of maturity of the industry, OEM partners will feel more or less attracted by the proposition. In the case of Intel, we have a clear example of where the ingredient brand programme has become so successful that Intel finds itself in a position of market dominance. Hardly any PC assembler can break through without carrying the Intel Inside logo. Intel's efforts have had positive effects in terms of PC sales. Another example, mentioned recently, is the deal between IBM and Dell. This deal has been praised by both sides; for Dell, there are obvious financial advantages (licence technologies instead of investing in R&D) and marketing advantages (differentiate and build competitive advantage by being first to market).

Strategic intent

What are the key competitive forces at play? In today's dynamic markets, changes happen at a fast pace. Ingredient branding decisions should be used as strategic tools to build barriers to entry. Along with product qualities, there is nothing stronger than capturing a customer's imagination to protect and grow a competitive position.

Does the technology fit into the strategic intent of the company? Before a company commits to branding a component it should investigate the fit with its future strategy.

Is this technology core to our future development? Do we want to be associated with the ingredient technology and the related applications? Although these questions seem bland, they are, however, the key to deciding whether or not a company is planning to brand its technology in OEM environments. It is then crucial to determine the position of the technology within the overall brand architecture and assign a clear value proposal to each constituent.

Is the company focusing on one stage of the value chain? For vertically integrated companies (partially or totally), ingredient branding can be highly risky. The risks of damaging brand equity, increasing consumer confusion and cannibalizing existing market share are not to be neglected. Sam Albert, an industry consultant, used the term 'co-opetition' for the strategy in which a company both competes and co-operates with rivals. This issue should be tackled both in the light of existing business models as well as the desired one. 'A company may decide to license a technology to others for manufacturing and distribution because it does not have the required capabilities itself' (Parr and Sullivan, 1996) but also if it has the strategic intent to refocus its resources on core competencies.

Business area and technology

Is the company focusing on one business area? Companies such as Monsanto, Akzo Nobel or DuPont de Nemours operate over a wide range of business areas. Given the wide stretch in their activity, any ingredient branding strategy should be designed taking into account the specificity of each business area, the role the ingredient brand will play in the overall brand architecture (core or peripheral) as well as the desired positioning

Does the company own a single technology or a portfolio? Like Intel or Dolby, Gore-Tex is a company that has built its reputation and its product quality on a narrowly focused offer and value proposal. Other companies have wider portfolios that stretch to different technology types. The brand strategy, in this case, will have to decide as to the type of umbrella required as well as to the technologies that will be bundled under a single brand.

Young's – Harry Ramsden's

The successful extension of a famous restaurant brand into the competitive grocery market.

Shell-Mex – BP

The use together of these famous brands created an impact which lasted long after the dissolution of the venture.

VISA
A famous and respected brand, used world-wide in co-branded card applications.

Lycra
DuPont's ingredient brand Lycra adds a strong quality endorsement for fabrics and garments which incorporate it.

Bailey's – Häagen-Dazs
For gourmets this co-branded match was made in heaven.

Tefal – Le Cordon Bleu
The prestigious Le Cordon Bleu name fits perfectly with Tefal's high quality Integral cookware range.

SWITCH
The reassurance provided by this symbol benefits both card holders and issuers.

Worldwide Fund For Nature (WWF)
A product which is co-branded with the world-famous WWF logo enjoys a greatly enhanced image.

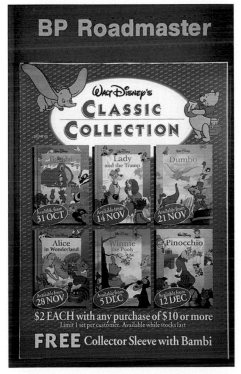

Disney – BP

The combination of these two brands results in an eye-catching promotion.

© Disney

Dolby*

An ingredient brand which represents high quality and technical excellence.

*"Dolby" is a trademark of Dolby Laboratories.

Exclusive Le Cordon Bleu
Culinary Cruises
1999 - 2000

SILVERSEA
ALL-INCLUSIVE, ALWAYS EXCLUSIVE

Silversea – Le Cordon Bleu

These co-branded cruises demonstrate that even the most luxurious product can benefit from an appropriate co-branded offer.

Nippon Ham – Le Cordon Bleu

The Le Cordon Bleu name reinforces the high-quality image of a range of Nippon Ham products marketed in Japan.

BP – Woolworths

One of the pilot sites for this recent retail partnership in New Zealand.

Cisco

Cisco advertise to Internet users, advising them to ensure that they choose an access provider who displays this logo.

CISCO SYSTEMS

EMPOWERING THE
INTERNET GENERATION[SM]

Teflon

Teflon appears upon a wide range of co-branded goods, signalling the substantial benefits brought by this amazing product.

TATA – BP

An exciting lubricants venture in India, where each brand benefits from the other's values.

Measures of the technological dimension in a portfolio are the breadth (range of technology types in the portfolio) and depth (number of patents in each technology area). ... Also relevant to the technology dimension are the relationship of technologies to current and future products, the degree to which technologies match the company's strategic plan and strategic intent, and the degree of technological focus (Parr and Sullivan, 1996).

Is the company's technology/technology portfolio mature or in its growth phase? Product life-cycle theory plays an important role in branding issues. A mature technology can be harvested (cost leadership or even outright sale), upgraded technologically or milked through a clever differentiation strategy.

> The people who market DuPont's chemicals and mineral products understand they have a considerable advantage because of the company's reputation for innovation, credibility and stability. Even if there is nothing particularly innovative about a specific product they might be selling, one manager acknowledged, 'people buy from us because we are DuPont.' That is the essence of commodity branding'. ('How to Brand Sand', in *Strategy and Business*, Second quarter 1998).

The stage of growth requires branding solutions that are flexible and can accommodate upgrades or new developments. Growth periods, generally, are characterized by fast pace of change, constant introduction of new technologies and short time to market. There is a 'need of a matrix to go fast to market in a cost effective way' (Strickland, 1994). Intel's example is a classic. As explained earlier on, Intel's initial strategy (the 1986 campaign) failed clearly to differentiate and led to high levels of confusion in the buyer's mind. The Intel Inside campaign managed to establish a clear and customer-driven (not technology-driven) message in the consumer's mind. By not focusing on specification, Intel has built an umbrella for future development

Next, How?

The branding issues here come from general branding theory. Based on internal analysis, customer analysis, industry and competition analysis, the brand can be built on sustainable and hard-to-replicate differentiation. The elements that are covered here are the particularities for ingredient brands.

Brand foundation

The ingredient brand needs clear foundations (values). They have to be the basis for all manifestations of the brand and will allow coherence and clarity.

Brand architecture

What are the relationships between corporate and service-business lines, products and ingredient technologies? What are the values at each level? What do you keep and what are you committed to give up?

We can see that the more specialized and narrowly focused the value proposal, the more monolithic the brand. On the other hand, the more diversified and the more vertically integrated the company, the less monolithic it will be. There is a thin line between these two extremes (monolithic and stand-alone): this is the line of endorsement.

Endorsement can take various forms:

- Visual endorsement.
- Naming structure endorsement.
- Addition of corporate name.
- Combination.

Moreover, the endorsement will deal with the required strategic level of branding. The choice will be then to focus on:

- A single technology (with potential future broadening of stretch);
- A set of bundled technologies;
- An umbrella for numerous technologies.

Based on the questions listed in the 'why?' section and on the company's vision and aspiration, the optimal brand architecture will be developed to make the ingredient both relevant and valuable to the mother brand. The migration strategy will then define the degree of endorsement over time as well as the potential evolution towards a stand-alone identity.

Brand positioning and value proposal

As the US advertising gurus, Ries and Trout, put it, 'positioning is what you do to the consumer's mind'. In branding technology, we are always faced with the perennial tension between technical features and consumer-driven benefits. Contemporary literature on this subject obviously favours the benefit-driven approach. It should be said that this really depends on the level of education of the customer, on cultural differences and on the overall brand strength. Issues to consider are as follows:

- Attribute positioning.
- Benefit positioning.
- Use–application positioning.
- User positioning.

- Competitor positioning.
- Product category positioning.
- Quality–price positioning (Kotler, 1997).

The positioning choice will have to be made taking into account the overall brand architecture and the relationship between corporate, service and product levels. The value proposal is the ultimate idea we want to leave in the consumer's mind that will best reflect the desired positioning.

Corporate identity

The way the brand manifests itself visually and translates the key values will be crucial to its success. Designed to build a consumer-facing profile, the ingredient branding will have to be inspirational and sustainable over time.

Brand management

There is no strong brand without a strong management and clearly defined foundations. Often overlooked, a great part of brand-building is generated by the coherence of the approach and the consistency of the effort. Behind every brand is a great idea, and a lot of sweat and faith.

In Conclusion

Ingredients are perhaps the original – and most potent – co-brand partners. Mention co-branding to laypeople and names like Gore-Tex, NutraSweet and, famously, Intel will spontaneously and eagerly be cited. Not only are ingredients the originals, they represent the most lasting and investment-specific areas of co-branding, when intermingling of company's technologies and trust is at its most intimate. This holds even more true with the increasing impact of 'disintermediation'. 'Branding will become more important in a remote delivery environment which offers more choice' (R H Evans, 1997).

Table 5.1 Overview of ingredient brands

Company	Ingredient brand	Link to parent brand	Value proposal
Dolby	Dolby	Monolithic	
Intel	Intel	Monolithic	Intel Inside
Gore-Tex	Gore-Tex	Monolithic (recent development of new endorsed trademarks catering for other needs)	Guaranteed to keep you dry
Cisco systems	Cisco	Monolithic	Cisco NetWorks
Motorola	DigitalDNA	Endorsement (DigitalDNA by Motorola)	It makes your television mindful
Monsanto	NutraSweet	Stand alone	The brand sweetener
DuPont de Nemours	Lycra	Endorsement (Lycra only by DuPont) – increasingly stand alone	The Lycra difference
Akzo Nobel	Sympatex	Light endorsement (Sympatex by AN) – increasingly stand-alone	Whatever you do stay dry
Lucasfilm	THX	Light endorsement (THX by Lucasfilm)	
Nike	Air-Max	Within brand environment	
Reebok	DMX	Within brand environment	
Sony	Trinitron	Within brand environment	
Mitsubishi	CDI	Within brand environment	

Bibliography

Books

Philip Kotler, *Marketing management*, 9th edition, (Prentice Hall International,1997).
Parr and Smith, *Valuation of intellectual property and intangible assets*, 2nd edition, Wiley, 1994.
Parr and Sullivan, *Technology Licensing*, Wiley, 1996.
Thompson and Strickland, *Crafting and implementing strategy*, 6th edition, Irwin, 1995.

Newspapers and Magazines

Financial Times
The Economist
Strategic management
Strategy and business

Notes

1 'Complementary assets are those assets and capabilities used to transform technology or innovations into revenue generating products ... they include tangible assets and capabilities such as design, high quality manufacturing, marketing, distribution, support services, and capital, as well as assets such as brand names and reputations.' (Parr and Sullivan, 1996.)
2 Cisco's brand strategy.
3 DuPont de Nemours has been included in this category, despite the fact that it is actually a supplier of technologies, because it obeys the dynamics of a multiple brand portfolio. Since we are looking at brand-related issues, we have to consider Dupont de Nemours's specificity. Its portfolio stretches from fibres to chemicals and through to pharmaceuticals.
4 Based on published DuPont research.
5 Based on internal launch brochure.

6 Legal Aspects of Co-Branding and Trademark Licensing

Bob Boad

A COMPANY's brand is usually one of its most valuable assets and authorizing a third party to use it, for example in a licensing or franchising arrangement, always requires careful consideration and control. However, in a co-branding situation a number of exceptional factors have to be taken into account and these may have important legal implications. This chapter sets out some guidelines on legal issues that may arise with co-branding but in all cases legal advice should be taken, as every co-branding venture is unique and will require specific adaptation of the general principles. Depending upon the nature of the products or services concerned and the countries in which they are produced and marketed, some additional considerations may also impact upon the project and require specialized legal advice that is beyond the scope of a book such as this.

The Co-Branding Agreement

The formal written agreement between the partners in a co-branding venture has a crucial role to play in ensuring a harmonious relationship between them and it can also help to ensure success. A well-written contract will not only clearly define the targets and facilitate the achievement of the objectives but will also help to prevent frictions and misunderstandings from arising.

Whilst it may sometimes appear expedient to launch a co-branding project with only 'Heads of Agreement' in place, the temptation should be resisted. There is no substitute for a detailed agreement which has been executed by both parties prior to the commencement of the venture and this should always be their aim. Controversial points are rarely easier to resolve if postponed and pressures of time from those keen to get the venture up and running should not be permitted to deflect the parties from settling the terms in advance.

However, the contract, no matter how well drafted, cannot make up for the choice of an inappropriate partner (see Chapters 3 and 8 for a more detailed discussion of this topic). Building brands can take time and so can building the relationship between the partners; moving towards long-term goals sometimes requires short-term compromises.

The basic role of the agreement is to set out in writing clearly and unambiguously what the parties have agreed, so that they understand exactly what they are permitted to do and what is prohibited or compulsory under the agreement. They will still need to have a great deal of trust in one another, since the agreement can never provide for every last detail or unlikely eventuality. The arrangements will need to give the parties the freedom to safeguard their respective brands and to continue to develop them separately, whilst providing adequate reassurance that the co-branding will not do anything that conflicts with or compromises the underlying core values of their brands. For example, in most cases each party will no doubt wish to rule out any similar co-branding deals with one of its competitors but in other cases this may be exactly what one of the brand owners intends – Intel's deal with many different computer manufacturers is an example of such 'multiple co-branding'– but in either case the point needs to be made clear to avoid misunderstandings and conflicts.

Where one or both brands will continue being marketed separately the proprietor may wish to provide for co-ordination of market positioning and advertising strategy for the brands, to avoid any embarrassing contradictory stances such as the co-branded product emphasizing its quality pedigree whilst one of the brands decides to adopt a low-price strategy to meet price-cutting competitors in its original market. Regular liaison meetings between the parties may be the most effective way of achieving this.

The parties will need to decide who is to have primary responsibility for marketing the co-branded product. It may simply be one of the partners, or it may need to be a new entity in the form of a formal partnership or joint-venture company. For example, where one of the brands is being used to brand an ingredient or component (the 'ingredient brand') which is used in the production of the other branded product or service (the 'dominant brand'), the parties usually decide that the best solution is the simplest one of giving the owner of the dominant brand the primary responsibility for the marketing of the co-branded product. The owner of the ingredient brand must place its trust in the continuing marketing skills of its partner but it does enjoy the advantage of sharing in the rewards without having to become involved in the day-to-day management of the co-branded business. Such an arrangement will minimize debate over minor points and should help to avoid damaging delay in responding to market developments.

The procedure for handling customer complaints deserves to be considered in detail, for this subject has implications for both brands, including any separate business which the partners may conduct under the brands, and it has the ability to cause consternation for the partners and for their customers. The partners need to be in close agreement on the policy to be pursued in relation to the resolution of complaints and it may also be advisable to ensure that this closely mirrors the policy which they apply in their independent business. If, for example, one partner enjoys a reputation for a 'no quibble, money-back' philosophy in its original business, there will be a natural tendency for customers to expect the same terms to apply if the brand subsequently appears upon a co-branded offer and any departure from that policy may disappoint consumers, bringing a backlash in both the co-branded and the original business.

The agreement should provide for regular reviews of the trading position and how the brands are being used, particularly if one of the entities is effectively managing the co-branded business and the other is not involved in day-to-day affairs. This not only prevents an undesirable development from progressing too far with one of the partners being unaware of it but also provides a mechanism for discussing and defusing issues that otherwise might develop and become a source of controversy.

The initial term of the agreement needs to be long enough to give the parties the confidence to invest in developing the co-branded product or service and believe that they will see a return. The agreement will usually commence with a fixed term during which neither party can withdraw, except where the other party commits a serious breach of the terms of the agreement or there is some other important development (such as the other party being declared bankrupt or being taken over). It is also usual to provide for termination in the event that the other party commits a less serious breach but then fails to remedy the situation within an agreed term. It is then common for the agreement to move on to an 'evergreen' phase during which it simply continues from year to year for so long as both parties are happy for that to happen but with either party being able to give an agreed minimum amount of notice of termination to the other if they should decide to end the relationship. The agreement must also set out the agreed course of action for the parties when the arrangement is eventually terminated. It is so much easier to agree sensible termination provisions at the start of a relationship than to postpone discussion of these until they are needed, as by that stage there may be some animosity between the parties and it is all too common for such disputes to become the subject of costly and time-consuming litigation or arbitration. It may seem rather negative and pessimistic to be discussing the end of the relationship before the venture is even under way, but a realistic approach must be taken and providing for an orderly exit is the only sensible course of action. It does not mean that the parties are any less committed to the success and long-term survival of the co-branding venture, it simply demonstrates competent and far-sighted management.

Post-termination details, such as title to customer lists and whether they may be used by one or both partners in pursuing their independent business, both during and after the term of the agreement need to be considered. Who upon termination will own and who may utilize any other databases, or any other potentially valuable assets created by the venture (such as copyrights, designs or trademark registrations for jointly developed packs or promotional materials, or information technology which has been created for the joint business) should be provided for in advance. It is even worthwhile agreeing whether or not the partners may make mention of their former venture: a party which is smaller and less known may be more enthusiastic to do so than a party which is larger and better established.

Title to Intellectual Property Rights

It is so basic that it may easily be overlooked or appear unnecessary but it is always worth checking that your proposed partner actually owns the brand that it is bringing to the venture and that it has bothered to register it for the goods or services which are to be relevant for the co-branding activity. This will help to avoid potentially serious misunderstandings if it turns out that the brand is actually owned by a parent company or perhaps even belongs to a third party who simply licenses the trademark to your proposed partner. Such a third party may take a dim view of the intended co-branding as soon as it finds out what its licensee is up to and demand that the sales cease immediately but this may not occur until after you have made a substantial investment in launching the co-branded product or service, so such checks are well worth making at a very early stage in the discussions.

It is also important to ensure that other types of intellectual property, such as patents, copyrights and registered designs belong to the proposed partner or, if they do not, to have assurance that the owner is in agreement with the proposed use in the venture. It is perhaps a good time also to conduct an audit of your own intellectual property rights and make sure that their formal protection is comprehensive.

It is all too easy to commission a new label or logo from a designer or have an advertising agency produce a distinctive new promotional campaign but forget to ensure that the relevant copyright is assigned to the client who ordered the work. Particularly close attention needs to be paid to this issue in respect of any materials produced on behalf of the co-branding venture.

Trademark Clearance

One of the most basic but vital requirements is to ensure that the trademarks are available for use in relation to the co-branding project. Although the venture will not often take either of the brands involved into new markets, in some cases the co-branded product or service may be offered in geographical markets where the proprietor of one of the brands has not previously operated by itself or it may expose one of the brands in additional market sectors within its traditional territories.

In either case it is important to establish at an early stage that the mark is free for use in relation to the co-branding application and where new countries or market sectors are involved it will be necessary to carry out searches of the trademark register *and* of the marketplace to ensure that there are no conflicting marks already registered or in use.

For trademark registration purposes, goods and services are allocated to one of a number of different classes and most countries have now adopted a common system, known as the International Classification of Goods and Services. For example, COURVOISIER is primarily used to brand cognac which falls in class 33 but before commencing to market a co-branded brandy sauce with SAINSBURY it would be prudent to conduct a search of class 30, which is the relevant class for such sauces, in case an unrelated third party owns independent rights in relation to sauces or similar foods for a mark which is identical or confusingly similar to COURVOISIER. The two entities owning such rights in the same or similar marks may have happily coexisted in their respective sectors of the marketplace for many years, perhaps without even being aware of the existence of one another, until the co-branding brings them into direct contact and perhaps even into head-on competition.

Even if the brand owner's primary product and the new co-branded product fall in the same class of goods it is still advisable to conduct such a search to ensure there are no unexpected obstacles to the plan. For example, BOVRIL beef extract is a class 30 product and so are potato crisps but prior to the launch of SMITH'S potato crisps flavoured with BOVRIL beef extract it would be prudent to check to ensure that there are no prior marks registered, pending or in use, which would conflict with the use of BOVRIL in relation to potato crisps. Such a clearance programme should not only include searches of the relevant classes of the Trade Marks Register but also extend to a check of the marketplace for use of any similar but unregistered marks. In many countries established use of a mark may give rise to enforceable 'common law' rights, but even in a country where unregistered marks do not enjoy such protection there may be strong commercial reasons for avoiding adoption of a mark that is similar to one which has already been used in the proposed new country or market sector. Similarly, a mark that had hitherto been used to brand a component part may, as a result of the new co-branding activity, need also to be cleared for use in relation to the complete product, or a service mark which is subsequently used in connection with a co-branded product may need to be searched for the relevant goods.

In certain circumstances it may be advisable to make some additional clearance searches on other registers or databases, for example by checking the local register of company names or business names, or by ensuring that there are no conflicting Internet domain names protected. In some fields it may be necessary to check a specialist list of protected names: for example the generic names of medicines are carefully regulated and a trademark which is being introduced into that field for the first time needs to be cleared for possible conflicts with the existing names on such list.

Trademark Registration

As indicated in the section above relating to checks that a trademark is free for use, co-branding deals may take a trademark into new market sectors or expose it in countries where it had not previously been used and so it is also vital that the portfolio of registrations keeps pace with these developments. Trademarks should be protected everywhere that they are used and in each of those countries they need to be registered in all of the classes of goods or services which are relevant to the existing use, or any future extension of activity which is proposed.

Co-branding may result in more complicated marketing arrangements and possibly limited 'hands-on' involvement for one of the brand owners, increasing the risk that sales of the product or service may be extended to new markets without the proprietor making equivalent additions to the trademark protection. Both brand owners have to ensure that they remain fully informed about the scope of the activity, even if one partner has no day-to-day responsibilities for marketing the co-branded product or service and regular monitoring of the marketing of the co-branded product or service is necessary.

David Castle, a UK trademark attorney whose clients include Le Cordon Bleu culinary academy, explains what this means in practice for a client's portfolio of trademark registrations:

> The breadth of activities, particularly the diversified co-branding activity ranging from cruises to delicatessen products and cookware to books, results in registrations of Le Cordon Bleu's trademarks being required in between 10 and 12 different classes of goods and services, depending upon the plans for a particular country. To fully protect a mark such as this requires regular liaison with the client to ensure that the

portfolio of registrations remains adequate. Ideally we like to receive warning of expansion plans at a very early stage in order that we may check to make sure the mark is free for use and still have time to get an application filed with the local Trade Marks Registry before the negotiations progress too far. It can take several years before an application works its way through to registration but normally this need not prevent the mark from being used meanwhile. It is also important to watch out for the need to prepare (and in some countries record) licences authorising any entities other than the registered proprietor who wish to use the trademark.

Parallel Imports

In some markets there is considerable unofficial importing of branded products, known as 'parallel imports' in Europe or 'gray goods'in the United States, and it is important to be vigilant for outbreaks of such activity, since this can take the co-branded items into markets where the brand owners did not intend them to be sold. It may cause particular difficulties if the positioning of the co-branded product in its country of origin is not compatible with its positioning in the destination market, or if there is a clash with the equivalent positioning of any products marketed separately under the brands in the destination market.

In some cases the brand owners may wish to prevent such parallel importing and the particular circumstances may enable them to do so. In cases where it is not desired to prevent such activity or where it is not legally possible to interfere, they must still remember to seek adequate protection of their trademarks, even though they are not directly or actively involved in the marketing of their co-branded products in that country. The exposure of their brands to local consumers could easily tempt a third party to try to register or to imitate their trademarks and if the brand owners have not thought to obtain adequate trademark registrations they may face considerable difficulty in preventing such mischief.

In some cases the parallel importer relabels or repackages the goods and such activity has given rise to much litigation, particularly within the European Union. Co-branded products could also be affected by such activity and if, for example, the parallel importer decided to increase the prominence of one of the brands compared to the original packaging (perhaps to take advantage of a greater reputation for that brand in the destination market), then the partners in the venture may wish to take legal advice to find out if such alteration can be prevented.

Trademark Licensing

A trademark licence is required where a trademark belonging to one entity is used in the course of trade by a different entity. Mere display of a mark – such as a retailer announcing in its window or its press advertising that it sells a particular product – does not require a trademark licence but where the user is doing something that alters the nature of the goods (such as cooking raw foods for supply through a quick service restaurant) or is doing something which has the potential to affect their quality – such as bottling beer which has been supplied in bulk by the brewer who owns the brand – then a licence agreement will normally be indicated. In appropriate cases this licence may form part of the agreements controlling a more comprehensive franchising deal.

Most co-branding projects will involve trademark licensing. At their simplest they will require one of the partners to license its brand to the other. Where a new joint venture entity has been formed they will each have to license it to use their marks. In some cases the parties will need to arrange for cross-licensing of their brands to one another, e.g. where each partner is actively marketing products or services bearing a mark belonging to the other.

Great care needs to be taken to define at the outset exactly what is being licensed to the co-branding venture to prevent disputes arising at a later date. Traditional marks such as words or logos, as well as less orthodox marks such as pack shapes, get-up (trade dress), colour schemes, musical 'jingles' and advertising slogans should all be considered for registration and inclusion in the schedules of marks covered by co-branding trademark licences, to ensure that the activity is properly controlled and use by the partner can be terminated cleanly at the end of the relationship. The schedule of licensed marks will need regular review to ensure that any new marks have been added.

As with all trademark licensing, it is essential that the owner of the mark concerned actively monitors and controls the quality of the products or services upon which its mark appears and in some countries it may be necessary to record the licence. Failure to attend to these requirements could endanger the enforceability, value or validity of the trademark. Normally each proprietor will wish to retain sole responsibility for dealing with any infringement of its trademark but it is advisable to confirm this in writing. Usually this will also mean bearing the cost of such action but it may be that in certain cases the partners in a co-branding deal agree to share the cost of such defending of one or both trademarks.

Trademark Royalties

In certain circumstances, payment of royalties may be an appropriate way to reward one of the partners involved in the co-branding activity, rather than adopting some other way of sharing the profits of the venture. For example, where one entity is actively managing the marketing of the co-branded product or service and the second entity is taking a less active role, it may be that a royalty payment is the easiest way to apportion the returns, rather than for them to try to agree upon a formula which gives an equitable split of the profits based on the perceived value of their respective brands and the other contributions that they are making to the venture.

Account may have to be taken of the marketing of the brands individually because promotion of the brands separately from the joint project could have spill-over effects on the sales of the co-branded product or service. Also, each brand will come to the co-branding venture with an existing worth and reputation which has been created by its past use and although this value will be the starting-point for the discussion about royalty rates or other sharing of profits, it will be the contribution which it is expected to add by participation in the co-branding venture that will be the main driver of the price to be commanded for its use. The co-branded sales will in turn affect the overall valuation of a brand – see Chapter 7 for a more detailed discussion of this topic.

Regular reviews of the rewards paid to the participants will be necessary to ensure that the payments remain appropriate in the face of their respective contributions to the project.

Taxation

Tax planning is an essential part of any business activity and the co-branding venture may have some implications for the tax position of one or both partners, so specialist advice should be obtained at a very early stage. It is important to ensure that potential liabilities (such as exposure to taxation in additional jurisdictions) and possible benefits (such as the ability to claim some tax relief or grants in respect of investment relating to the venture) are fully explored.

The temptation to hold the relevant trademarks offshore in a tax haven should be balanced against other considerations. Such an arrangement may, for example, require an extra layer of trademark licensing to facilitate the use of the mark in the co-branding venture and may have other implications, for example relating to the enforcement of the mark against infringers.

Competition Law Aspects

Depending upon the nature of the venture, the parties involved and the market being targeted, the proposed co-branding venture may require clearance by national or supranational competition authorities. Two entities who individually hold fairly strong positions in the relevant market sector may, by joining together in a co-branding venture, cross the stipulated threshold and require approval for their plans. Once again, it is vital that specialist advice is taken at an early stage.

A successful co-brander may find that it achieves such a strong position and reputation in the marketplace that it faces anti-trust actions brought by the authorities or legal action from companies who take objection to one or other aspects of its market power or business activity. For example, 'serial co-branders' (who routinely license many of their customers to co-brand using their mark) may find that a would-be user of their mark who is prevented from doing so retaliates by litigating.

In one case, brought in the US against Intel, the judgment ordered Intel to continue supplying their technical information and products to the plaintiff because their technology was so ubiquitous that it might fall within the legal definition of an essential service, without which no computer company can do business. Such a statement is at once both flattering and worrying for a brand owner, as it threatens their ability to choose the parties with whom they trade and to whom they license the use of their trademark and other intellectual property rights.

Product Liability

Participation in co-branding projects may raise important issues of product liability for the owners of the brands, particularly if the activity falls outside their usual field of business. If the co-branding exposes a brand owner to new geographical markets or to new market sectors it may involve unexpected risks and may not be covered by existing insurance cover, so, at the very least, additional protection may need to be arranged.

Indemnities from the partner may also be appropriate, particularly for a brand owner who is venturing into unfamiliar countries or market sectors where it cannot adequately assess the risks involved.

Care may also need to be taken in deciding which entity within a group of companies is most appropriate to participate in a risky co-branding venture, to avoid placing the group's mainstream assets directly at risk. The decision in such matters is always difficult and in any event most reputable brand owners would be very reluctant to allow an unsuccessful co-branding venture to fail, leaving dissatisfied customers behind, because of the potential knock-on effects on the image and value of their brand in its other markets.

Development of New, Jointly Owned Intellectual Property

Co-branding requires great discipline in relation to the use of the existing equities in the brands. Control is also required over any development of new intellectual property rights otherwise friction may arise; for example there may be disputes over proprietorship of the new creation, or the continuing validity and distinctiveness of the individual brands may be threatened by shared property which draws heavily on one or both of them.

If a new mark, get-up, musical jingle or slogan is developed exclusively for use in relation to the co-branded product or service, then the parties will need to agree on how best to protect it and how to control its use. For example they will have to decide whether or not to register it, if so who is to own it, how the protection of it will be funded and what will happen to the mark in the event that the co-branding venture is terminated. The difficulties which arise with such mutual property may lead them to decide to limit, or even to avoid entirely, the development of same and instead continue to rely upon the clearly defined properties contributed by their respective brands.

In particular, the development of a 'hybrid' mark or get-up, incorporating elements from both 'parent' brands, is something that should be avoided as it will tend to weaken both of the brands upon which it draws. Such blending together of the property of the two parties will damage the distinctiveness and may make it easier for third parties also to adopt marks that are similar to one or other of the 'parent' brands. See also the comments in Chapter 3 on the risks and pitfalls of co-branding activity.

Proper Use and Acknowledgement of Trademarks

When trademarks are used upon packaging or in advertisements it is important to distinguish them from the surrounding text and identify them as being trademarks. This helps to build up recognition that they are trademarks, prevent unintentional infringement by third parties and aid their protection and enforcement, especially in countries such as the USA where failure to give such notice of a trademark's status can result in no award of damages against a party who infringes it.

In a co-branding situation the proper identification of trademarks and attribution of them to their respective owners is particularly important. It should be made clear to customers and to traders whether something is a trademark and which of the parties owns it; confusion is something to be avoided as it could threaten the validity of the mark(s). The observation of a few simple rules can prevent any such confusion from arising and put the co-branded product or service in a stronger position to help tackle any unfair competitors. Figure 6.1 opposite sets out some guidelines for proper use of trademarks.

Failure to enforce proper use of a trademark in co-branding applications exposes the mark to unnecessary risks. If a mark is used in a manner that

Some general principles for correct use of trademarks in co-branding applications	Examples	
1. A trademark is an **adjective** – it describes the particular product or service that is branded by it. This means that wherever possible each trademark used on a co-branded product or service should be followed by the common name for the particular product or service, for example: BOVRIL beef extract and SMITH'S crisps.	'we only use lycra in our jeans.'	**WRONG**
	'our jeans contain LYCRA spandex fibre.'	**RIGHT**
2. A trademark is not a noun so it should **not be used in the possessive form.**	'you will see from PREDICT's analytical results'	**WRONG**
	'the results of the PREDICT analysis service'	**RIGHT**
3. Each trademark should be **distinguished from surrounding text** by presenting it all in block capitals, a contrasting typeface, or at least with an initial capital letter.	'the quality of smith's potato crisps'	**WRONG**
	'the quality of SMITH's potato crisps'	**RIGHT**
4. **Acknowledge** all trademarks on labels and in advertisements and promotional material but do not claim they are registered trademarks (e.g. by using ® symbol, unless you are sure that is the case in the relevant country or countries and for the particular goods or services to which reference is being made.	The 'Intel Inside' logo and 'Pentium are registered trade-marks of Intel Corporation; 'Quantex' is a trademark of Quantex Systems Inc.	**RIGHT**
Acknowledgement of unregistered marks may be done in various ways: e.g. by using a statement or by using an asterisk after the mark together with a footnote, or by using the two-letter trademark symbol (or its local equivalent).	ENERGOL* engine oil (with footnote: *ENERGOL is a trademark of BP Amoco p.l.c.)	**RIGHT**
	ENERGOL™ engine oil (with footnote: ENERGOL™ is a trademark of BP Amoco p.l.c.)	**RIGHT**
5. One trademark should not be used to **prefix** the other.	'this IBM Pentium computer ...'	**WRONG**
	'this IBM computer features a Pentium microprocessor ...'	**RIGHT**

Figure 6.1 Guidelines for proper use of trademarks

suggests it is descriptive or the common name for one of the component parts or ingredients in a finished product, then there is a danger that it will become a generic term which is free for all traders to use, rather than its proprietor retaining the exclusive right to control its use. See the 'Lycra' case study in Chapter 3 for further insight into the risks and how to respond to them to prevent the loss of a valuable trademark.

The use of one brand name to prefix another is inadvisable as it can make it more difficult to protect them, even in situations where the marks both belong to a single proprietor. Many brand owners succumb to the temptation to put their 'masterbrand' or 'house mark' in front of the sub-brand used for a particular product or service but this can help to reinforce the perception that the second mark is a generic term that all are free to use, particularly where the second brand is lacking in distinctiveness. In the UK case involving a dispute over the use of the term 'Oven Chips' the judge held that the manner in which McCain had used the name, prefixed with their masterbrand, had contributed to the perception that it was a generic term and he refused McCain's request to curtail its use by competitors.

In a co-branding situation, where the brands belong to different proprietors, the practice of prefixing one with the other is even more objectionable and can result in the two marks eventually being seen as a single 'hybrid' mark. This confusing situation can impact upon the ability of the proprietors to enforce their rights and in some circumstances the practice may even threaten the continuing validity of the individual marks.

7 | Creating Economic Value Through Co-Branding

Jan Lindemann

T HE ULTIMATE purpose of the co-operation of two or more brands is the creation of economic value. Although all types of co-branding situations described in Chapter 1 have been established to create economic benefits for all participants, the financial measurement and valuation of these benefits is a very complex matter. To make the principles and applications of the valuation of co-branding structures more transparent, this chapter will for the most part focus on the visible co-operation of two independently owned brands in the sale of a new product or service with its own identifiable earnings stream.

The synergy of the combination of brands relates to the creation of awareness as well as the complementing and strengthening of brand equities. The synergies of the co-operating brands create economic value that should be higher than the value these brands could create in the same market individually. The economic value creation of brands in a co-branding structure can be assessed through financial valuation techniques.

Defining the Co-Branding Structure

Co-branding can be found in a variety of structures. From a valuation standpoint, most co-branding structures fall into two main categories which we will call Major–Minor and Equals.

Major–Minor

Major–Minor defines a co-branding structure in which an established brand is supported by a minor brand to provide specific equities which the major brand does not possess but which have a sufficiently significant impact on the sale of the co-branded offer. It is important for the Major–Minor structure that the minor brand could not sell the co-branded product or service under its own brand.

97

A typical major–minor structure can be found in ingredient branding where an ingredient brand such as Intel or NutraSweet supports, with specific equities, the offer of the established brands such as Compaq, IBM and Diet Coke. Although NutraSweet is enhancing the sale of the co-branded Diet Coke–NutraSweet cola drink the brand could not sell such a product solely under its own brand name. A different major–minor structure exists between credit- and payment-card brands and bank brands. The major payment-card brands such as Visa, MasterCard, Discovery and Switch are supported by the brands of the issuing banks which provide minor support by connecting the payment card with the customer account. Although the issuing banks have sufficient equities for establishing a payment card by themselves they lack the credibility of the payment-card brands with respect to national or international acceptance.

Equals

Equals defines a co-branding structure in which both brands are equally poorly or strongly established and both brands could potentially provide the product or service under their own brand. Both brands co-operate because the synergies regarding brand equities and investments promise to create a co-branded business that will yield both parties a higher return than offering the same product or service under their individual brands. Examples of such structures are payment or credit cards offered by an airline, department store or utility in co-operation with a financial service institution. British Airways and Diners Club engage in co-branding of credit cards to enhance mutual brand equities as well as to complement the equities of their brands. The British Airways brand has previously not been involved in financial services but has, through its airline operations, developed sufficient equities (trust, service quality, familiarity, etc.) to credibly offer such services to its customers. In co-branding with Diners Club it seeks to strengthen the credibility of its credit card offer. The Diners Club brand is established in credit cards but lacks the familiarity and customer base of the British Airways brand. British Airways and Diners Club could each offer a single branded credit card. However, both brands have decided to co-brand their credit card offer because the economic benefit of this co-operation is perceived to be higher than the benefit that could be derived from a single branded offer.

Independent of the structure, the value creation of the co-branding structure is also affected by the exclusivity of the arrangement. The value creation is higher in situations in which the arrangement is exclusive as typically found in food ingredients. However, co-branding can become a commercial necessity for creating brand value. The Intel brand, for example, has achieved a position in which computer manufacturers feel obliged to co-brand with it in order to be in the consideration set of potential buyers. A similar relationship exists between credit-card brands and the card-issuing bank brands.

Creating Economic Value

The value creation of co-branding can be recognized in any or all of the following five areas:

1. Sales volume,
2. Sales price,
3. Operating costs,
4. Marketing investment,
5. Brand risk.

Sales Volume

Co-branding creates a sales volume in a specific market that could not be achieved by each brand individually. The creation of sales volume can be achieved through either awareness or enhanced brand equities or a combination of both. Major–minor structures tend to focus on enhancing brand equities while equals structures tend to utilize both features. In the major–minor structure the co-operation of two brands can increase share in markets in which one of the brands is already established. The minor (ingredient) brand adds equities to the co-branded offer that affect customer choice and thus increase unit purchase and market share of the co-branded offer. This is typically the case in markets in which the product offer is not strongly differentiated by price. As co-branding is a relatively new development the number of prominent examples is limited. Good examples are food ingredients in snack foods, cereals and soft drinks.

To illustrate, for a period of time Coca-Cola sold its Diet Coke with the branded ingredient NutraSweet because the company believed that this co-branding exercise would result in higher-volume sales. The proven brand equities of NutraSweet supported the Diet Coke offering with a trusted sweetener. When Coca-Cola tried to change the sweetener and sold Diet Coke without the NutraSweet co-branding, sales volume was immediately affected.

Sales Price

Co-branding can also directly affect the selling price of the co-branded product or service. Pricing arrangements of co-branded products and services are kept secretly and very little is publicly disclosed. A prominent example for the effect of co-branding on the sales price of a co-branded product is Intel. Intel Corp. estimate that the 'Intel Inside' co-branding with the computer manufacturers has added about $150–$300 to the retail price of a computer. It can be assumed that there are several cases in which co-branding has resulted in a higher sales price.

Operating Costs

Co-branding can create a level of demand that reduces the operating costs of the co-branded business through economies of scale and significantly lower marketing costs. If, for example, the co-branding of a product results in a significantly higher sales volume, operating costs could be reduced through better use of existing production capacity and lower procurement costs for raw materials. Ongoing marketing expenses can be kept relatively low as the co-branded offer benefits from marketing activities of each brand in its main markets. The co-branded venture can potentially benefit from lower operating costs and thus from a higher operating margin than a single branded venture.

Marketing Investment

Co-branding can significantly reduce the marketing investment for the co-branded business. If the co-operating brands are well established the co-branded business will not require large up-front marketing investments. Accrued and on-going marketing investments in each of the co-brands' established markets will contribute to the value creation of the co-branded offer.

There are situations in which one of the co-brands is not established and requires significant marketing investment. Examples are ingredient brands such as Intel and NutraSweet which have been created as brands only through co-branding. In these cases the initial marketing investments have been substantial – although presumably less than they would have been had Intel or NutraSweet tried to build their brands without co-branding.

Brand Risk

Co-branding also affects the risk assessment of the earnings generated by the co-branded offer. Overall, the risk profile of the co-branded offer should be lower than that of the same offer only sold under one of the brands, that is the earnings forecast is more certain. The risk of the co-branded offer can be reduced by an increase in awareness, perceived product quality, leadership through innovation or premium pricing, marketing support and geographical spread. However, there can be situations in which co-branding can enhance risk instead of reducing it. This refers to situations in which one of the brands faces a catastrophic crisis such as pollution, poisoning or technical defect. Less obvious but potentially more damaging can be the long-term decline of one of the co-brands through negligent brand management.

Using Brand Valuation to Assess the Value Creation of Co-Branding

In a co-branding arrangement each company involves one of its most valuable assets, its brands. The financial impact of co-branding can potentially be more important than operational joint ventures as there is a mutual flow of equities between the co-operating brands, not only in their joint venture but also in their core markets. This means that companies involving their brands in a co-branding structure have to evaluate both the anticipated financial benefits from the co-branded venture and its effect on their brands in their main markets.

Brand valuation is a formidable management tool for assessing the risks and benefits from involving a brand in a co-branding structure. As brand valuation provides a financial assessment it facilitates both the decision on and management of the participation in a co-branded venture. It provides answers to the key areas of management concern:

1. Whether or not to enter the co-branded venture.
2. How to select the most appropriate partner brand.
3. How to allocate the profits between the co-operating brands.
4. How to determine the shareholdings in the venture.
5. How to split the initial marketing investments.
6. How to assess the impact of co-branding on the brands' core markets.

Choosing the Appropriate Valuation Method

Several valuation methods have been used in the past to value brands. These include cost-based valuation approaches such as historic and replacement costs, multiples of branded sales and operating profits, as well as capitalized future earnings of premium prices and the relief from royalties.

The premium price method is mostly used for the valuation of ingredient brands for which a direct price comparison to a generic commodity product is possible. Certain food ingredients and computer chips are traded as commodities. In such situations one could argue that the price difference between a branded ingredient and a generic product would represent the value of the brand. Many major–minor co-branding situations are sometimes settled in that way. The supplier of the ingredient brand (minor) is compensated through the sales price of the ingredient to the OEM supplier (major) and not through a profit share of the co-branded operation. In the past, this approach has been applied to many ingredient brands. However, we believe that the increased use of co-branding, in particular amongst Equals, requires a more sophisticated approach for assessing the value each brand adds to the co-branded offer. In addition, companies have become more aware of the value of their brand assets and seek to ensure that they receive a fair return for involving them in a co-branded venture. Assessing a return for each of the co-brands requires an in-depth understanding of the economic value creation of each brand in the co-branded venture. This can only be achieved through economic value-based valuation approaches.

The most widely accepted and recommended brand valuation approaches are based on the 'economic use method' which is the only method that complies with the principles of current corporate finance theory. The economic use method assesses the value of the brand by identifying the brand's future earnings and discounting these to a net present value using a discount rate that reflects the risk of those earnings being realized. Amongst the economic use methods Interbrand's approach to brand valuation is the most widely recognized and accepted methodology. This is particularly true for the valuation of co-operating brands as the Interbrand approach has the flexibility to identify the value contribution of each of the individual brands.

Interbrand's Approach to the Economic Use Method

Interbrand's concept of brand value is based on the premise that a brand (when well managed) influences customers' purchase decisions in a way that creates an economic benefit for the brand owner. Brands provide their owners with a security of demand (and thus of earnings) that they would not enjoy if they did not own the brand.

The value of a brand is reflected not only in the amount of earnings it is capable of generating in the future, but also in the likelihood of those earnings actually being realized. A brand valuation exercise comprises three elements:

1. Preparation of a forecast of the expected Net Sales and Economic Earnings of the co-branded business.
2. Identification of the importance of the role that each brand plays in driving demand for the co-branded business in order to determine Brand Earnings for the co-branded offer as well as for each of the co-brands.
3. Assessment of the risk profile of expected Brand Earnings to determine the appropriate discount rate for calculating the net present value of the Brand Earnings of the co-branded business.

Applying Interbrand's Valuation Approach to a Co-Branded Business

Forecasting Economic Earnings

The starting-point for assessing the value creation of a co-branding structure is the preparation of a financial forecast. If one of the brands already has an established position in the market to which the co-branding structure is intended to be applied, it is advisable to take the historic financial performance as a basis for forecasting. This forecast may be the strategic business plan or the management accounts and should ideally cover a period of 5–10 years. The financial forecast should be sufficiently detailed to include major profit-and-loss and balance-sheet items. The purpose of the financial forecast is to establish the expected Economic Earnings of the co-branded venture.

The Economic Earnings represent the earnings which are solely attributable to the intangibles of the co-branded business. The notion of the economic earnings is similar to value-based management models such as Stern Stewart's EVA (Economic Value Added) concept for the measurement of business performance. Economic Earnings are derived by subtracting from the Net Sales of the co-branded venture all operating costs which are necessary to generate these sales, a charge for the capital employed in the co-branded business and all applicable taxes.

In most businesses the capital employed comprises net fixed assets such as property, plant and equipment and working capital. Until a return is made in excess of what one would expect from the fixed assets and working capital tied up in running the business, it cannot be said that the brand (or indeed any other intangible) is adding value to the business. After making a fair charge for the capital employed, the residual earnings represent the prospective Economic Earnings of the branded business. These earnings would be equivalent to those generated by the business if it did not own any of its tangible assets and instead leased them from another party.

Deriving Brand Earnings

Brand Earnings are derived by identifying the portion of Economic Earnings that is solely attributable to the co-operating brands. This is achieved through the Role of Branding analysis. In some heavily branded businesses (such as perfumes or packaged foods), most of the Economic Earnings will be attributable to the brand as there are no other significant intangibles in the business. In more technically complex businesses, the ability to earn a profit in excess of a base return on the tangible assets is only partly a function of branding. It is much more so of other intangibles such as patents, technologies, expertise, sales forces, databases and distribution agreements.

The role that branding plays will vary between brands. For a single brand it may also vary between product categories, within a product category and between different countries.

Generally, the role that a particular brand plays in generating demand for the co-branded products and services will depend on a variety of factors, for example:

- the degree to which price is the determinant in selling the product;
- whether the consumer perceives it to be a high value-added or a commodity product;
- whether the consumer is highly knowledgeable about the product through previous experience with the product;
- whether the product is perceived to be technically distinct from competitors or generally interchangeable.

Interbrand has developed a process for examining these situations and estimating the degree to which the continued ownership of the brand is an intangible driver of demand for the branded business. By identifying the key drivers of demand for the branded products and services we are able to calculate what would be lost if the brand were lost as an asset of the business. This measure is referred to as the Role of Branding Index. This analysis is based on market research and market observations.

Before assessing the role of branding index for each of the co-branding brands it is necessary to assess the overall role of branding index of the co-branded offer. The following process is conducted to determine the role of branding index:

1. Identify the main drivers of demand in terms of what is prompting customers to buy the co-branded product rather than competing products.
2. Weight the importance of these drivers of demand in relation to each other.
3. Within each driver consider the relative importance of the brand versus other intangibles in making that driver effective. An assessment is made of how much the effectiveness or success of each driver would be undermined in generating demand if the brand were absent. The Role of Branding varies depending on the importance of the perception of the driver versus factual delivery of the driver. The perception element of the driver is usually communicated by the brand.
4. Evaluate the overall weighted Role of Branding in each driver and express as a percentage.
5. Consolidate the Role of Branding for all of the drivers and thus calculate the overall weighted Role of Branding for the co-branded offer.

To illustrate how the Role of Branding Index is derived let us assume the co-branding of two food brands for a new product. One brand is established in breakfast cereals, the other in snack bars. The co-branded product is a cereal snack bar that combines the equities of both brands. Market research has shown that the cereal brand could not offer a credible snack product under its own brand. The snack bar brand could credibly offer another snack bar product but lacks credible brand equities in the health and cereals area. We further assume that the co-branding arrangement is exclusive and neither brand will be used in another cereal snack product. Our case is therefore a major–minor situation in which the snack bar brand is the major brand and the cereal brand is the minor brand.

In Table 7.1 we have outlined a hypothetical role of branding index calculation for the co-branded venture.

Table 7.1 A role of branding index calculation

Demand drivers	Weighting	Dependence on (co-) branding	Role of (co-) branding
	%	%	%
Perceived quality	45	85	38
Lifestyle promise	25	100	25
Pricing	15	0	0
Familiarity	10	100	10
Promotions	5	70	4
TOTAL	**100**		**77**

Source: Interbrand

By applying the role of branding index to economic earnings, brand earnings are derived for the co-branded business. According to the above example the co-operation of both brands would account for 77 per cent of the forecast economic earnings. The remaining 23 per cent of economic earnings are attributable to intangibles other than the brands.

Attributing Brand Earnings to the Co-operating Brands

Once the overall brand earnings of the co-branded venture are identified we can assess the brand earnings attributable to each of the co-operating brands. For that purpose we use again the role of branding analysis. The split of brand earnings is derived differently for major–minor and equals co-branding structures. In a major–minor co-branding situation we extend the role of branding analysis by examining the effect of the removal of the minor brand to the co-branded role of branding index, for example, what percentage of brand earnings would be lost without the minor (or supporting) brand.

In our example we would assess the brand earnings that would be lost by removing the cereal brand from the co-branded cereal snack. The role of branding index calculation would then be as shown in Table 7.2.

According to Table 7.2, 55 per cent of economic earnings would be attributable to the major brand and 22 per cent of economic earnings would be attributable to the minor brand.

In a co-branding structure among equals the allocation of brand earnings would be determined in a slightly different manner. Since both brands offer similarly strong equities one would first assess the individual role of branding indices and assess the split of the brand earnings of the co-branded offer on the basis of the percentage contribution of both brands to the sum of the individual role of branding indices. Such a calculation would be necessary to account for the overlap in equities which both brands could claim to bring to the co-branded venture.

Through the role of branding analysis we can thus identify and quantify the specific equities that each brand contributes to the co-branded business. The role of branding analysis is also an excellent tool for assessing the potential partner brand. It shows whether the co-operating brands are complementary or overlapping for any of the drivers of demand. This allows us to assess the fit for any two proposed co-brands.

Table 7.2 A role of branding index calculation for a major–minor co-branding structure

Demand drivers	Weighting	Dependence on co-branding	Role of co-branding	Contribution of major brand	Contribution of minor brand	Role of major brand	Role of minor brand
	%	%	%	%	%	%	%
	A	B	C	D	E	F	G
			A × B			D × C	E × C
Perceived quality	45	85	38	70	30	27	11
Lifestyle promise	25	100	25	75	25	19	6
Pricing	15	0	0	0	0	0	0
Familiarity	10	100	10	70	30	7	3
Promotions	5	70	4	80	20	3	1
TOTAL	100	–	77	–	–	55	22

Source: Interbrand

Assessing Brand Risk

In order to calculate the net present value of the expected future brand earnings of the co-branded venture, we assess the risk profile of the brand earnings and determine the appropriate discount rate. If two brands offered the same amount of future earnings, but one was a strong, reliable, market-leading brand and the other was a recently launched, fashionable, relatively unproven brand (say, *Lego* versus *Tamagotchi*), the value of the first brand would be greater than the value of the second. This is because the value of a brand reflects not only what earnings that brand can be expected to generate in the future but also the likelihood of the brand being able to meet that promise. The difference in the risk profile of the same brand earnings forecast is reflected in the appropriate discount rate that represents the difference in brand risk.

Brand risk is assessed through the brand strength analysis. Brand strength is determined by comparing each brand to a 'notional ideal brand' according to seven attributes. The 'notional ideal brand' carries a slightly higher investment risk than government bonds which are regarded as the lowest risk investment.

The seven key attributes that determine the strength of a brand and thus the risk profile of its earnings are defined as follows, each with a maximum score:

- *Market (10).* This attribute assesses the market in which the brand operates according to its size, growth prospects, volatility and barriers to entry.
- *Stability (15).* Stability is assessed according to the brand's longevity, the perceived quality of its products and services, brand awareness and customer loyalty. In addition, we make an overall assessment of how the brand has endured competitive.
- *Leadership (25).* This attribute looks at how the brand influences its market. It takes into account the brand's market share, whether the brand can command distribution and/or a price premium and whether the brand is perceived to set the main trends in the market in particular with respect to innovation, new product development and major price points.
- *Trend (10).* Here we assess the overall long-term trend of the brand and its ability to remain contemporary and relevant to customers. One of the measurements is the development of the brand's market share over time.
- *Support (10).* This attribute assesses the marketing investments made in the brand. This includes size and consistency of marketing spend as well as the long-term consistency of the brand message.
- *Geography (25).* Here we look at the brand's general capability to cross cultural and national barriers and in particular its ability to generate earnings in different geographical market. This assessment also influenced by the importance of the geographical markets

- *Protection (5)*. This attribute assesses the legal protection of the brand as whole and of all its elements.

Applying the brand strength analysis to our hypothetical major–minor co-branded venture we can score each brand individually as well as the co-branded offer according to the above outlined framework:

Table 7.3 Brand strength score

Attributes	Major brand	Minor brand	Co-branded
Market	5	4	5
Stability	13	12	13
Leadership	18	15	19
Trend	6	5	6
Support	8	7	8
Geography	20	18	21
Protection	5	5	5
TOTAL	**75**	**66**	**77**

Source: Interbrand

The combined strength of the co-branding brands should result in a higher brand strength and thus lower risk for the co-branded offer than for either of the brands individually. The brand strength score of the co-branded venture reflects the synergies of the co-operation of both brands. The synergies can be identified by each scoring attribute. In our example the major brand is stronger than the minor brand. The attributes in which the major brand is significantly stronger are leadership and geography. Our example assumes that the co-operation of both brands creates an overall stronger branded offer. The synergies of both brands focus on the attributes stability, leadership and geography. The co-branded offer has a higher perceived product quality and awareness. It is also regarded as a leading brand in the new category and also benefits from a better penetration of different geographical markets.

In addition to the role of branding index the brand strength score is another tool for assessing the synergies from the co-operation of two brands. The combination of two brands does not automatically result in a higher brand strength score for the co-branded offer. The combination of a strong credit card brand such as American Express with a relatively weaker airline brand such as South West Airlines could result in weaker co-branded credit card. The co-branded credit card could be weaker in attributes such as stability and leadership. The brand strength attributes are an excellent checklist for assessing the suitability of a co-branding partner. If the brand strength Score of the co-branded venture is lower than the score of the stronger brand a co-branding may not be advisable for the stronger brand.

It is the brand strength score that reflects the relative security or risk profile of future brand earnings and which thus determines the discount rate to be applied. A strong brand provides a high level of confidence that brand earnings will be maintained and results in a lower discount rate. Conversely, a weak brand gives a lower level of confidence in future earnings, so the discount rate must be higher to reflect the increased risk.

The range of risk rates reflects the economic conditions of the market in which the brand is being sold. It will therefore be derived from risk-free rates (e.g., government bonds) and the cost of capital. The range set by Interbrand assumes that the ideal brand scoring 100 out of 100 is still slightly riskier than a risk-free investment and so commands a slightly higher discount rate. The riskiest brand (scoring 0:100) is discounted to infinity and the 'average' brand (scoring 50:100) is discounted at a level that is broadly in line with the average performance of branded goods companies. A low score reflects a high risk resulting in a high discount rate. A high score reflects a low risk resulting in a low discount rate.

The brand strength score determines the discount rate for the srand earnings of the co-branded venture as well as of each brand individually. In addition to the role of branding analysis the brand strength analysis provides a selection of key criteria against which a partner brand for a co-branded offer can be assessed. The analysis measures the contribution of each brand to each element of the brand strength of the co-branded business.

Deriving Brand Value

The brand value of the co branded venture is derived by discounting the expected future (co-) brand earnings with the appropriate discount rate, reflecting the combined brand strength of the co-brands. On the basis of the brand value calculation of the co-branded venture we assess the individual value contribution of the co-operating brands.

First, we apply to the brand earnings portion attributable to each brand (see role of branding index) a discount rate based on the brand strength score of each brand. Remember that the brand strength score of each brand will be lower than that of the combined score. That means that the risk profile of future brand earnings and the resulting discount rate of each brand will be higher than the brand strength score and discount rate of the co-branded brand earnings. The sum of the brand values of each brand will be lower that the brand value of the co-branded venture. The difference in brand value is the result of the difference in the brand strength score and thus in the applied discount rate. We can therefore allocate the difference in brand value to each brand on the basis of its contribution to the overall brand strength score.

We assess the brand strength gap between each brand and the combined brand strength. We add the brand strength gaps and divide the brand strength scores of each brand by the sum of the brand strength gaps. This gives us the proportional contribution of each brand to the combined brand strength. We allocate the difference in brand value according to this proportional contribution. The brand value of each brand in the co-branded venture is represented by the sum of the individual brand values and the allocated portion of the brand value gap.

The following example demonstrates the brand value assessment:

Table 7.4 Brand value asessment

	Major brand	Minor brand	Co-branded venture
Economic Earnings Forecast			£100m
Role of branding index			77%
Contribution by each brand	71%	29%	100%
Role of branding index	55%	22%	77%
Brand earnings	£55m	£22m	£77m
Brand strength score	75	66	77
Difference in brand strength score between each brand and co-branded offer	2	11	–
Discount rate imputed from brand strength score	11%	13%	10%
Brand value	£45m	£15m	£70m
Brand value gap			£7m
Brand strength contribution	11	2	13
Allocation of brand value gap	85%	15%	–
Additional brand value	£6m	£1m	£7m
TOTAL BRAND VALUE	**£51m**	**£16m**	**£77m**

Source: Interbrand

According to our example the total brand value of the co-branded venture amounts to £77 million of which £51 million would be attributable to the major snack bar brand and £16 million would be attributable to the minor cereal brand.

Brand valuation provides a detailed financial assessment of the value creation of co-branding. The technique allows the calculation of the overall brand value of the co-branded venture as well as the brand value contribution from each brand. Brand valuation comprises an excellent framework for assessing the synergies between co-operating brands.

Benefits and Risks

Brand owners engage in a co-branding structure because they believe that the co-branded venture will provide both parties with an economic benefit that they would not receive if they were to enter such a market by themselves. The benefits of co-branding are twofold. First, there are the obvious financial rewards from the co-branded venture. Second, there are additional benefits such as enhancement and transfer of brand equities from the co-branding partner as well as an increase in awareness.

While management tends to focus heavily on the benefits of co-branding the risk of such a venture is often underestimated. The transfer of brand equities and increased awareness can have a significant negative impact if one of the co-operating brands faces serious quality problems or disasters such as pollution or poisoning. The deterioration of one of the co-branding partners can affect not only the co-branded venture but potentially also the brand of the other partner. It is therefore advisable to weight benefits and risks carefully before entering a co-branding relationship. Brand valuation can help management in assessing the benefits and risks of a potential co-branding structure with respect to the co-branded market as well as the brand's core market.

Applying Brand Valuation to Managing Co-Branding Structures

Brand valuation is the appropriate management tool for managing a co-branding structure. It enables the co-branding partners to assess the value creation of their brands in the mutual venture and to manage that value with respect to the co-branded business as well as the brands' main businesses.

Brand valuation provides useful tools to assess the benefits and risks of entering a co-branded venture. The combination of financial analysis, role of branding index and brand strength score enables the co-branding parties to identify and quantify these benefits and risks. We can assess the economic benefit that each party derives from co-branding and compare it to the effect that co-branding could have on each of the brands' main markets. Brand valuation assists management in the decision whether or not to enter a co-branded venture. The main tools of brand valuation – in particular the role of branding index and the brand strength score – help management in selecting the appropriate co-branding partner.

Assuming equal investments of the co-operating brand owners in the tangible asset base of the co-branded venture brand valuation can be used to allocate the dividends between the partnering brand owners, determine the shareholdings of the partners and assess the initial marketing investment contribution. In addition, brand valuation can be used to assess the impact of co-branding on the brands' main markets. This makes brand valuation a valuable tool in the initial management decision on entering a co-branding relationship.

8

The Future of Co-Branding

Tom Blackett, Bob Boad, Paul Cowper and Shailendra Kumar

Time present and time past
Are both perhaps present in time future
And time future contained in time past.

TS ELIOT

You can never plan the future by the past.

EDMUND BURKE

Men must pursue things which are just in present,
and leave the future to divine Providence.

FRANCIS BACON

IF THREE such savants cannot agree on the predictability of the future, then what chance have we? 'Futurecasting' is, very clearly, never easy to do, and for this reason rarely a fruitful occupation. It seems hardly appropriate, however, to conclude this book on co-branding without some attempt to forecast what the next few years may have in store. There is every indication that increasing prosperity – particularly in Asia and Latin America – will continue to drive worldwide economic growth well into the next century. But who will benefit from the explosion in consumer demand? Will it be the big 'global' suppliers of goods and services? Or will we see resurgence in smaller national companies, which in turn become the regional and multinational groupings of tomorrow? Much will depend on political and societal factors: critically the extent to which the 'enterprise culture' model is embraced by developing countries; and whether, and how, public attitudes towards big corporations change.

Whatever the dynamics of change we believe that three things are as certain as anything can be in this uncertain, unpredictable world. The first is that 'speed to market', in a time of constant and accelerating change, will become a massively important competitive attribute. The second is that scarcity of resource will increasingly hamper the ability of any one company – operating in isolation – to grasp and exploit the opportunities available in a timely way. The third is that joint ventures, alliances and mergers will feature even more prominently as a way of enabling businesses to achieve the two preceding requirements.

This being so, then it is unlikely that we will see less co-branding in future – quite the opposite in fact. What interests us is how the process of co-branding strategy will evolve, who the future exemplars of co-branding will be, and what lessons there are to be learned from other forms of business 'partnering' – specifically the world of mergers and acquisitions. Let us start with M&A, in many ways the 'big brother' of co-branding.

Mergers and Acquisitions

Mergers and Acquisitions activity in 1998 broke all box office records, with the value of transactions exceeding a staggering $2400 billion. This contrasts with the previous era of frantic M&A activity in the late 80s – when the total value of transactions was around $500 billion. There are other differences too. In 1998 there were two-and-a-half times the number of transactions than at the end of the 80s, yet the total value of these transactions increased fivefold. This suggests that the average value of each transaction has doubled in the last 10 years. This is not altogether surprising, for two reasons. First, the increasing value of intangibles and brands are now accepted as the most important assets in any organization. In 1988 a study by Interbrand demonstrated that intangibles accounted for 56 per cent of the market capitalization of the leading UK companies, which together make up the *Financial Times*–Stock Exchange 100. Ten years later in 1998 this had grown to a remarkable 71 per cent (see Figure 8.1). Secondly, the huge increase in stock market-value has seen a paradigm shift in the M&A landscape. Whereas in the 80s 'cash was king', in the 90s equity reigns supreme allowing companies to pay for one another by the mere exchange of paper.

The largest deals are now approaching the $100 billion mark. The Exxon–Mobil merger will capitalize the merged entity at $80 billion with the earlier merger of Travelers–Citicorp valued at $72.5 billion. We have seen mergers that are astonishing not just for the size of the finances involved but also for the sheer complexity that accompanies this degree of magnitude. Contrast this with the largest takeover of the 80s, chronicled in the book *Barbarians at the Gate*, which described the $31 billion leveraged buy-out of RJR Nabisco by Kravis Kohlberg Roberts. There is another dynamic at work here. While the 80s boom was characterized by hostile takeovers, the 90s M&A activity has been characterized by consenting parties. The barbarians that were once at the gate appear to have been tamed, welcomed ... and invited in.

The reasons to engage in M&A activity may be one of several: from increasing market power by economies of scale, to acquiring critical mass, improving distribution and penetration or even eliminating the competition. Many are defensive moves for sheer survival when an industry consolidates. Ultimately, though, the rationale behind M&A activity is to increase shareholder value. This is done in two ways: either by creating value by realizing cost synergies, or by realizing revenue synergies. Naturally, the principle is that when two entities unite the whole is greater than the sum of its parts. In takeovers the value creation for an acquirer depends on the excess of the synergies delivered and sustained over the price paid for control of the target. It seems simple enough. The truth, however, is quite different.

A number of studies have concluded that most deals are less than successful. A study by McKinsey concluded that deal costs were recovered within 10 years

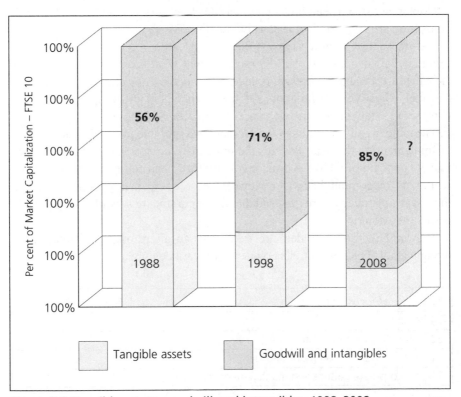

Figure 8.1 Tangible assets, goodwill and intangibles, 1998–2008
Source: Interbrand

in less than a quarter of all transactions. They further went on to report in their 1993 study that almost three in every five deals did not even earn back the cost of capital. By any of today's economic metrics this suggests that 60 per cent of deals were in fact value destroying.

In our experience, the fervour surrounding mergers and acquisitions activity has often masked one of the critical factors which could ensure the success of any corporate marriage. Mergers and acquisitions are regularly conceived out of an accounting-based approach to business where synergies, be they cost or revenue, are the predominant focus of value creation. The reason, however, why many mergers have failed to create shareholder value is that they have ignored at their peril the synergies between their respective customer, brand and employee profiles. It is essential to understand existing customer and employee relationships, to own the line of communication with them, to migrate those relationships to the merged organization and to use the power of the corporate brand to engender a greater degree of customer and employee loyalty in the merged business. It is through this process that a market-facing business can ensure future success.

Comprehensive research of European M&A activity conducted by KPMG's consulting arm reported some startling results. The report finds that there was a post-transaction review to assess the success of the merger or acquisition in less than half of all deals. KPMG reported that what seems to matter most is 'whether a transaction appears to have been successful rather than whether it has met objective benchmarks'. Of the 45 per cent of companies that did conduct a review the results were as noted in Table 8.1 below.

The table highlights much of the problem. Merger integration lies at the heart of implementing the deal. Perhaps the most instructive statistic is that in more than 90 per cent of all M&A deals involving European companies there was no marketing or communications review. In these companies it is probable that there was no strategy to review and that the same statistics would be applicable across the Atlantic.

The 'soft factors' in a deal are frequently an afterthought – if they are a thought at all. There is sufficient evidence to warn dealmakers that these factors

%	Area of focus/review	% of all M&A deals
54	Finance	<25
22	Staff/organizational structure	<10
21	Marketing and communications	<10
11	IT, corporate culture and management methods	<5

Table 8.1 Results of post-M&A reviews
Source: KPMG

are ignored at their peril. The proposed GlaxoWellcome and SmithKline
Beecham merger foundered over a clash of personalities at the top of the two
organizations, while Price Waterhouse and Arthur Andersen failed to come
together through profound and irreconcilable differences in corporate cultures.
Switzerland's Ciba-Geigy and Sandoz did merge successfully but chose a
different corporate branding approach by changing their name to Novartis. This
provided the opportunity to forge a new, forward-looking culture that this
affords – as a critical factor in this. Similarly, due consideration of the attitudes
and loyalties of customers need to be taken into account. When Lloyds Bank
merged with the Trustee Savings Bank it conducted a very thorough review of
branding strategy before announcing the name and identity of the new group.
Lloyds and TSB branches would remain in each of their heartlands, Lloyds in
the south and TSB in the north and Scotland. Gradually a new type of physical
identity has emerged for the group with a distinct Lloyds and a distinct TSB
part but with a shared back office. Lloyds TSB, the corporate entity, has not
alienated any of its customers by forcing them to transfer their loyalties to
another brand. Customers therefore continue to associate with one of their
brands rather than both. As Peter Ellwood, the then head of Retail (and now
Chief Executive) said in an interview with Retail Banker (19 January 1996) at
the time of the merger:

> A winning organisation knows that shareholder value starts with the customer. If
> you look after the customer well, you need staff to have an empathy with the
> customer, who realise they are in a service industry and who want to serve ... The
> exciting thing isn't just about cutting costs. The really challenging thing is about
> meeting customer needs and growing the income.

Lloyds' merger and customer integration policy has served them well. In 1998
the group headed the banking sector in terms of shareholder value creation, and
was third overall in the UK.

The parallels with successful co-branding are many. But the chief lesson
perhaps is that deals that are put together based purely on the compatibility of
the tangible assets involved, and which ignore the fit of the softer assets – be
these to do with customers, culture or brand – risk jeopardizing long-term
competitiveness.

Co-Branding Strategy

It strikes us that some of the very best and most successful co-branding ventures
have added considerably to the reputation of both brands concerned. We need
only look at the apparent indispensability of Intel as an ingredient brand: it

seems no serious PC manufacturer can nowadays afford to compete without 'Intel Inside'. Intel lends credibility to the PC brand and provides massive reassurance to the potential purchaser. The 'host' brand benefits through association with Intel and Intel benefits through association with the host brand (and the additional advertising exposure this brings).

We feel that, in future, companies planning to engage in co-branding activities will increasingly adopt more systematic processes for identifying 'brand' partners and strategies for mutual brand enhancement. We believe that co-branding in its 'purest' form has at its core the exchange of values or attributes (on a reputational level) between the brands, to create a new reality whereby both brands are perceived to be better as a result of the initiative. But how can this be achieved?

In any situation where two brands are made visible alongside each other to identify a new product or service, the values embodied by each brand can be expected to cross-fertilize the other. If this cross-fertilization is successful then the brands will benefit. This exchange, however, needs to be managed, and objectives need to be established at the outset of any initiative in order to ensure that the exchange is meaningful and mutually beneficial.

The planning process must therefore commence by defining the brand's values. This can sometimes be difficult but the use of a 'brand blueprint' can be helpful. Based on customer research and internal management workshops, the brand blueprint helps to identify and explore the whole range of values that characterize the brand. Once these values are identified they are sorted according to the following categories:

- Core values – the values that lie at the brand's heart and define the brand's emotional and rational reason for being and differentiate it from the competition.
- Absentee values – the absentee values the brand lacks but wishes to acquire.
- Peripheral values – those values which are inappropriate or negative and should be shaken off.
- Generic values – the 'tablestakes' or entry requirements which enable the brand to enter the category and compete effectively.

In addition to helping to define and categorize the brand's values, the brand blueprint process can provide important diagnostic information on how the brand can be developed; this comprises:

- Key brand supports – these are the emotional and functional elements of the brand which underpin the core brand values.
- Core brand proposition – the brand's *raison d'être* – the core brand

promise which the brand owns in the consumer's mind.

- Brand essence – the distillation of the brand proposition and values – the ultimate promise to the customer.
- Brand personality – how the brand would be expressed – should it have human characteristics?
- Brand tone of voice – how the brand speaks to its stakeholder audiences.

Diagrammatically the brand blueprint appears as shown in Figure 8.2 below.

Clearly, undertaking a brand blueprint exercise enables the brand owner to become intimately acquainted with its brand. With experience it is possible to use the blueprint to judge potential partners, and when a list of such candidates is drawn up a blueprint can be created for each to evaluate which offers the greatest potential for enhancing the brand.

The process for identifying potential partners, based on the blueprint and objectives, can proceed in a series of steps:

Step One: From the strategic objectives that have been set for the brand certain assumptions can be made as to which market category, territory and level of premium the co-branding initiative should involve in order to yield

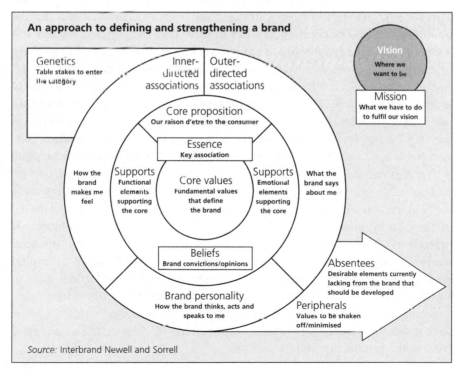

Figure 8.2 Interbrand's brand blueprint

the best results.

Step Two: Taking the hypothesized co-branding environment from Step One, create a separate list (using the brand blueprint) of reasons why the brand might be desirable within these scenarios.

Step Three: Generate a list of third party brands that might benefit from these 'desirable contexts'.

Step Four: Remove all brands from the list that fall outside the requirements (in terms of market category, territory and premium position) of the strategic objectives.

The resulting list creates, effectively, the 'brand marketplace' within which a suitable brand partner can be sought.

Whilst up to this point we have only considered initiatives from the point of view of the 'hunter', it is important to be aware that as the practice of co-branding becomes more commonplace brand owners can expect to be 'hunted' too. Where this is the case it is possible to scrutinize the prospective partner using the brand blueprint process; however, if the sought-after brand is in great demand (as is Intel) it is useful to develop a formalized version of the system – a bespoke 'brand screening system', if you will.

An example of a typical screening questionnaire is contained in the Appendix. This is designed to reflect the key strategic and partner criteria that must be met to indicate a go/no go decision. It seeks to score both the potential partner and the proposed initiative through measures such as market bias and objectives, branding implications, timeframe, brand resonance and media exposure.

The score which results from the screening acts as a form of 'desirability index' for the venture. This can be calibrated to some extent by running either previous or hypothetical case studies through it, but it is important to understand that any 'pass marks' or hurdles must be flexible, as there are no absolute scores. A better way to use these scores is as a measure of relative benefits between different initiatives.

This technique for identifying and screening co-brand partners is a sophisticated one. But it needs to be. Brands these days are sophisticated, based as they are on a subtle blend of values and attributes. Yet the technique is probably no more complex than the procedures managements and their financial advisors would undergo when assessing technical compatibilities or capital requirements. Considering the importance of brands and the difficulties that can surround the successful consummation of a co-branding relationship, using such a technique as a means of risk reduction seems only sensible. It would also be wise to use these techniques to measure the effects of co-branding on a regular basis as the venture continues.

Future thoughts

It seems to us that much best practice in co-branding has emerged from the high-technology sector. As this sector, which is massive and still on an exponential growth path, has many famous brands, it is instructive to learn how a company like IBM regards co-branding. The following is drawn from their co-branding guidelines:

> IBM is engaged in a broad range of collaborations with other companies, across the industry and worldwide. These relationships afford us opportunities in emerging and changing markets. If undertaken carefully, these collaborations can broaden our access to new markets, improve our responsiveness and strengthen our positioning and brand relevance. Because of our size and complexity, it is critical that we undertake these collaborations pro-actively and with full consideration of their strategic implications.

This overview by IBM covers in a concise and appropriate way many of the key points about co-branding we have tried to make in this book. In fields such as credit cards, computer software and hardware, the Internet and many other hi-tech industries, co-branding is already established as the norm and it is the stand-alone offer which may in the future come to be considered as unusual. We expect many of the hi-tech, fast-growing markets to demonstrate particular affinity for co-branding and increasingly sophisticated consumers not simply to relate to and understand co-branding offers but to actively demand them. The busy customer of the future will be seeking immediate reassurance that a product or service will perform and brands will play a huge role in the rapid decision-making process.

Elsewhere, in more 'traditional' co-branding areas, we may be seeing a levelling off in growth. In the US credit card market in 1998 co-branded cards grew at an annual rate of 20 per cent, while non co-branded cards grew by only 8 per cent (according to *Credit Card Management*, 21 January 1999). However, there are signs that some card issuers are exploring alternatives to co-branding. For example, issuers such as Capital One, First USA and MBNA are going it alone with 'lifestyle' cards. In this way, they are assuming the role hitherto played by their co-brand partner, retaining all the revenues and providing the focus for relationship building with their customers.

So what does the future hold for co-branding? In our opinion it still has plenty of scope for further growth and development. It will find applications in new roles and in ever more fields – in relation to services as well as upon products. Increasingly brand owners will consider it as an additional option for growth and evaluate it against traditional 'brand extension' activity. As additional market sectors become increasingly difficult to penetrate for newcomers, co-branding may be preferred as a faster, cheaper and safer alternative growth strategy.

As product counterfeiting and imitation becomes ever more widespread many brand owners will recognize that establishing truly global use of their trademarks may be the best way of securing them against piracy and ensuring that the strongest possible legal rights are created at the local level to deal with such problems. The low-capital option of brand licensing, especially through co-branding agreements, will inevitably find favour in many cases as few corporations have the resources and 'reach' to operate global operations single-handedly.

A strong local partner in a joint venture may in the future be more likely to recognize the value of its own brand and reputation and seek a prominent 'on pack' role for its brand rather than settle for a relatively anonymous role as a traditional low-profile licensee marketing an international brand.

We may see co-branding practice mimic the marketplace and itself become more sophisticated and segmented. For example, we will almost certainly see more carefully focused and measured 'recipes' for co-branding deals. As the concept of co-branding becomes ever more widely used and acceptable the list of potential partners will grow and a would-be co-brander will not be satisfied if it finds interest on the part of just one leading brand in the target sector but will increasingly discover that almost all of the brands are willing to consider potential partners for co-branding ventures. In the same way that other marketing tools such as advertising and sponsorship have been adopted over the years in new fields (e.g. banking, contraception, religion) or by companies who once eschewed them (e.g. Marks & Spencer) so co-branding will come of age as a truly mainstream marketing activity.

We may also see the emergence of brokers who will seek to bring together compatible brand owners; such agents may work either on their own initiative in spotting suitable 'marriages' or on behalf of one brand owner who is seeking another but who lacks the resources, the skills or the inclination to track down and evaluate a partner for itself.

There may be other interesting developments to come. We may see further attempts at 'unauthorized co-branding', of the type already seen in some of the cases involving repackaging of parallel imports (gray goods). For example, Orifarm, a parallel importer who was repackaging Boehringer pharmaceuticals for the Danish market (rather than simply re-labelling the original packs in the local language, stating who the importer was, etc.) added its own mark prominently to the new packs. Boehringer complained that the effect of the repackaging was to imply that the product was an Orifarm product and the Maritime and Commercial Court of Copenhagen agreed, although the decision is the subject of an appeal.

Similarly we may see large retail chains becoming increasingly assertive in requiring special co-branded packs of leading brand name products (see 'Increased Risk of Lookalikes' section in Chapter 3), rather than pursuing the supermarkets' tactic of recent years in developing 'lookalike' own-label products which mimic the get-up of the brand leader in an attempt to send out a message of 'equivalence'. Brand owners may find themselves coerced into consenting to such initiatives rather than risk the loss of an important outlet for their goods, in much the same way as many grocery brand owners have felt inhibited from tackling supermarkets that have launched even the most blatant copies of distinctive branded pack get-ups.

But let us leave this subject for now, perhaps to return in a few years time when many new and exciting developments are bound to have taken place in the world of co-branding.

Appendix

Co-branding Screen

The following screening process is intended to be used to identify the (relative) brand benefit of one, or more potential projects

Please note that, when selecting a project, the brand benefit is only one of a range of ways in which a project may be of value.

Instructions for Use

Please answer all questions unless the screen requests you to skip forward.

The questions within the screen fall roughly into 2 categories:

- *Open questions which may require extended answers*
  In this instance please detail your answer and reasons

- *Questions where the answer is either yes / no or a numerical score*
  In this instance please fill in the answer boxes on the form.

Where questions award a score, please multiply the number(s) corresponding to the relevant answer(s) and multiply this by the overall question weighting number which is at the top in bold. For example, if the question is:

Is 3rd party attractive for future branding reasons?   **3**

- If no, go to question 13; if yes, are they, for example:
  - Genuinely Caring (customer focused/ethical)?   4
  - Always Innovative (dynamic/progressive/entrepreneurial)?   4
  - Totally Reliable?   3
  - Quick to react?   3
  - Committed?   3
  - Expert?   5
  - Successful?   5

                                                          Question Score   ☐

If the third party is considered to be *both* committed and genuinely caring, then the score would be 21, which is calculated like this:

> committed (3 points) + genuinely caring (4 points) = 7.
> This is then multiplied by the question weight (in bold at the top),
> which in this case is 3 ($7 \times 3 = 21$).

For the final score please add all question scores answered.

Section 1 – What 3rd party?

1. Are you proactively looking for an alliance with a 3rd party?

   no ☐ Please skip to section 2

   yes ☐ Go to question 2 within this section

   For the remaining questions within this section please detail your responses on a separate sheet of paper.

2. (Screening Research – proactive) What brands and companies are currently active within this business area?

3. (Screening Research – proactive) What brands do you think could benefit from moving into this business area and why?

   - What companies have the right kind of brand values for the area, but are not present?
   - Is there any learning to be gained from companies who have previously failed to enter the market?

4. (Screening Research – proactive) When selecting an alliance company you will also need to consider what benefits they offer the project other than brand benefits:

   Operational strength and size
   Geographic considerations
   Technological expertise
   Other – please document

5. (Screening Research – proactive) On the basis of the above 3 questions, summarise a list of 3–5 companies which you feel will meet your objectives

Section 2 – Initial Checklist

1. Is this a market in which there are specific problems with progressing the brand?

   no ☐ Please continue to co-branding section (section 3, page 5)

   yes ☐ Please detail what you think these problems are

   Do you think the brand could embark upon this project under a different guise?

   no ☐ Reject

   yes ☐ Please detail what brand name you would anticipate using, and refer to Marketing Manager

2. Is the 3rd party likely to reject the alliance on financial grounds?

   no ☐ Continue to question 3

   yes ☐ Can you make the offer more attractive?

   　　　yes ☐ Detail how and refer to Marketing Manager

   　　　no ☐ Reject

3. Does 3rd party have any brand values which could adversely affect the image of your brand e.g. overtly criminal/political etc.?

   no ☐ Please continue to question 4

   yes ☐ Please detail what these values are, and how they could affect your brand and refer to the Marketing Manager before continuing.

Section 3 – Brand Fit – 3rd Party and your brand

Please be aware that this screen solely considers branding issues which may affect a potential project. All other market and operational issues affecting the project's viability should have been considered internally. Please ensure as a final check that all considerations raised at the start of this document have been explored.

Please note that a quantity of background work will need to have been done in order to complete this section.

Please fill in the blank brand blueprint for the 3rd party attached, the definitions for the different areas are:

Core Values: those values that lie at the heart of the brand and make it different to the competition at a functional and an emotional level.

Key Supporting Values: all other supporting brand values.

Generics: threshold and rational values, which are necessary to allow the brand to compete.

NB – Generics are values which it is necessary to have in order to exist in the marketplace, but which must not be overemphasized because of the need to achieve differentiation.

Desired Values: those qualities desired but not possessed.

Negatives: qualities and values which are to be shaken off or minimized.

Brand issues affecting viability of the project

1. Could the brand values of the potential 3rd party damage the reputation of your brand?

   - Are they involved with any other businesses whose reputation you think could be potentially damaging to your brand?
   - Is there any negative media (or other) speculation about the company?
   - Have any of their recent ventures failed publicly?
   - Are there any perceived/reputed concerns over liquidity/gearing / operational dynamics?
   - Could you anticipate any problems with their senior management?

   If the answer to any of the above is yes, please list the possible threats separately and refer to Marketing Manager.

Which 3rd party?

2. What brand values is the 3rd party perceived to have? What brand values will it be perceived to have in the future?

   Create brand blueprint for 3rd party
   (Core values are current and future values central to brand identity. Peripheral values are undesirable current associations)

   - What are the core values?
   - What are the core competencies?
   - What are the peripheral values?

   Consider the possibility of hidden strategies for the brand which may alter its positioning – is there any reason to suppose these may exist? Please detail.

   What weaknesses are there within the 3rd party brand values? Please list these, detailing how they could affect this project.

   Outline action points for your brand and/or 3rd party which address these weaknesses.

3. How do the brand values of the 3rd party interact with yours? **5**

   - Does one or more of 3rd party core values oppose core values of your brand?   −5
   - Does one or more of 3rd party core values oppose peripheral values of your brand?   4
   - Is one or more of 3rd party peripheral values opposed by core values of your brand?   1
   - Does one or more of 3rd party peripheral values match peripheral values of your brand?   −5

   Question Score ☐

4. Is 3rd party attractive for future branding reasons? **3**
   If no, go to question 13, if yes, are they, for example:

   - Caring?   4
   - Innovative?   4
   - Committed?   3
   - Quick to react?   3
   - Reliable?   3
   - Expert?   5
   - Successful?   5

   Question Score ☐

5. Does the 3rd party brand have the desired positive high profile
   and by exposure from a consumer perspective: **3**

   within intended geographic area?   score between: 1–3
   within intended business area?   score between: 1–3

                                          Question Score   ☐

6. Are there any branding implications for an existing 'alliance' of
   this new project which are significant/prohibitive? Are there any
   similar implications for any of your brand's sister businesses or
   corporate centre? If yes

   ● In what way would this new alliance branding overlap with
     any existing alliance brands?   **4**
   ● if competitive (similar brand in similar market)?   –1
   ● if dangerous (other alliance brand threatens to damage
     either your brand or the new alliance brand)?   –5
   ● if complementary (reinforcing or enhancing your brand through
     other relationships)?   2

   If there are any implications, i.e. if a score is awarded for this
   question, please refer to the Marketing Manager.

                                          Question Score   ☐

   Refer any cases with negative scores to Marketing Manager.

   **Please also refer any cases where planned or named *future*
   alliances may be affected to Marketing Manager.**

7. Is 3rd party attractive for current branding reasons?   **4**
   If no, go to question 8, if yes is this:

   ● reputation for expertise?   5
   ● reputation for trustworthiness   score between: 2–4

                                          Question Score   ☐

8. Is this project: **3**

- Likely to increase significantly and measurably the awareness of your brand(s)' within the target markets? 3
- Increasing your brands' perceived credibility within new products or markets? 4
- Intended to involve initially your expertise and a 3rd party brand with the intention of ultimately introducing your brand? 4
- Financially profitable? 2
- None of the above? 0

Question Score ☐

If the score for question 8 is 0, refer to Marketing Manager.

If this motivation is solely financial, (i.e. the question score is 6) please state how you can 'own' the project? Can brand benefits be introduced over time? **Refer analysis and conclusions to Marketing Manager.**

9. Are there any existing/planned 'alliances' of the 3rd party or affiliates that may affect your brand?
   If no, go to question 11; if yes:

   - Please list any known, existing or planned alliances.

Alliance Company	Type of alliance

If any of the above alliances involve a direct competitor, refer to Marketing Manager.

Alliance Considerations:

10. Are any of these potential/actual alliances opposed to these values of your brand? **4**

    - Caring −4
    - Innovative −4
    - Committed −3
    - Quick to react −3
    - Reliable −3
    - Expert −5
    - Successful −5

Question Score ☐

- Where there is a negative score, could the 3rd party be persuaded to curtail/amend alliances in interest of its alliance with you?

  - Is it anticipated that the proposed alliance with you is more important than these other alliances? Can you make a convincing case for this?

  - Construct and attach an action plan for counteracting potential conflicts.

- Where the alliance has negative brand values but another alliance / affiliate company is of merit, can we re-start with them?

  yes ☐ res-start the screen

  no ☐ please end here

Refer all cases with a score of less than 0 to Marketing Manager.

- Are any of the potential 3rd party's possible alliances with one of your competitors?

  If yes, refer to Marketing Manager.

Why is your brand attractive for 3rd party?

11. Why is your brand attractive to 3rd party and/or its owners?   **2**

    - Money   1
    - Reliability   3
    - Operational size   3
    - UK awareness/visibility   5
    - Stability   2
    - British   1
    - Future /vision   5

                                          Question Score ☐

                    Total Score for Screen: ☐

Source: Interbrand

Glossary of Terms

Acquisitions/Mergers These involve the coming together of two organizations. The two either form an entirely new organization (a merger) or one party absorbs the other (an acquisition).

Alliance Intended as a generic, unspecific term including all forms of relationships or associations with a third party.

Brand A brand is a mixture of attributes, tangible and intangible, symbolized in a trademark which, if managed properly, creates value and influence. 'Value' has different interpretations: from a marketing or consumer perspective it is 'the promise and delivery of an experience'; from a business perspective it is 'the security of future earnings'; from a legal perspective it is 'a separable piece of intellectual property'.

Brand associations (1) The feelings, beliefs and knowledge that consumers (customers) have about brands. Brand positioning is about shaping and controlling these associations. (2) When an association is deemed relevant and useful it is termed a brand value.

Brand earnings The share of a brand-owning business's cashflow that can be attributed to the brand alone.

Brand equity The strategic – or competitive – benefit to the brand owner of owning the brand. Distinguishing qualities of the brand that inform consumer choice.

Brand extension Leveraging the values of the brand – in food and drinks usually the tangibles, but in luxury goods the intangibles – to take the brand into new markets. Difficult to do well.

Brand identity The brand's 'reason for being' (see Brand Platform) – its sense of purpose – and the 'clothes' it wears to help it express this.

Brand image The customer's net 'out-take' from the brand. For users this is based on practical experience of the product or service concerned (informed impressions) and how well this meets expectations; for non-users it is based almost entirely upon uninformed impressions, attitudes and beliefs.

Brand management Practically, this involves managing the tangible and intangible aspects of the brand. For 'product' brands the tangibles are the product itself, the packaging, the price, etc. For 'service' brands the tangibles are to do with the customer experience – the retail environment, interface with salespeople, overall satisfaction, etc. For product, service and corporate brands the intangibles are the same and include brand identity, advertising and brand personality.

Brand mission What the brand owner must do to bring its brand vision to life (see Brand vision). Benetton's mission is 'To make the world aware of the stupidity and senselessness of war, racism, sexism, pollution, bigotry and discrimination or prejudice'. Apple's is 'To help man change the way he works, learns, thinks and communicates'.

Brand parity A measure of how people perceive products of a given category that are sold under different brand names. Brand parity varies widely from one category to another. It is high for petrol, for example: about 80 per cent of respondents (BBDO survey) see no real difference between brands. By contrast, brand parity for cars is low: only about 25 per cent of respondents say that one make is much the same as another.

Brand personality The attribution of human personality traits (seriousness, warmth, jolliness, etc.) to a brand as a way to achieve differentiation. Usually done through long-term above-the-line advertising and appropriate packaging and graphics.

Brand platform A brand's DNA, its unique defining qualities. These qualities are supplied through tangible attributes and intangible values (see below and also Brand mission and Brand vision).

Brand positioning (1) Creating a set of expectations in the mind of the consumer. (2) A deliberate pattern of actions that a company adopts to give its brand a distinctive position compared to other brands and ensure that individuals in the target market can tell that brand apart from others. The first step is to make sure that the company's own employees understand the brand promise and brand position.

Brand strategy A plan for the systematic development of a brand to enable it to meet its agreed objectives. The strategy should be rooted in the brand's vision and driven by the principles of differentiation and sustained consumer appeal. The development of a brand strategy often leads to a communication strategy which goes beyond visual identity.

Brand valuation The process of identifying and measuring the economic benefit – brand value – that derives from brand ownership.

Brand values Attractive qualities that define the brand's promise. Values are functional ('what the brand does for me'), expressive ('what the brand says about me') and intimate ('what the brand and I share at a fundamental level').

Brand vision The brand's reason for being. By extension, what the world would miss if the brand was no longer around. Benetton's vision is 'Discrimination or censorship of any brand will not be tolerated'. Apple's is 'Man is the creator of change in this world. As such he should be above systems and structures, and not subordinate to them'.

Branding Selecting and blending tangible and intangible attributes to differentiate the product, service or corporation in an attractive, meaningful and compelling way.

Co-branding Bringing together two or more brand names in support of a new product, service or venture.

Consumer product Goods (consumer goods) or services (consumer services) purchased by an individual for private use or for other members of the household.

Core competencies The collective learning in an organization. The knowledge, experience and capabilities that contribute most to a company's ability to compete.

Corporate identity The corporation's 'reason for being' (see Brand platform) – its sense of purpose – and the 'clothes' it wears to help it express this.

Country of origin The country from which a given product comes. Customers' attitudes to a product and their willingness to buy it tend to be heavily influenced by what they associate with the place where it was designed and manufactured.

Customer characteristics All distinguishing, distinctive, typical or peculiar characteristics and circumstances or customers that can be used in market segmentation to tell one group of customers apart from another.

Customer service Anything that creates customer satisfaction in connection with the purchase, delivery and use of a product or service. This includes courtesy, attractive shop premises, and speed and precision in meeting commitments, but does not include services that are part of the product.

Demographics The description of outward traits that characterize a group of people, such as age, sex, nationality, marital status, education, occupation or income. Decisions on market segmentation are often based on demographic data.

Differential product advantage A feature of a product that is valuable to customers and is not found in other products of the same category.

Differentiation Creation or demonstration of unique characteristics in a company's products or brands compared to those of its competitors.

Differentiator Any tangible or intangible characteristic that can be used to distinguish a product or a company from other products and companies. A brand can be a powerful differentiator in itself if it is properly managed.

Endorsed brand Generally a product or service brand name that is supported by a masterbrand – either dominantly e.g. **Tesco** Express or lightly e.g. Nestlé **Kit-Kat**.

Franchising The granting of a contractual licence by the franchiser to the franchisee which allows the latter to perform specific activities, but where the franchiser provides assistance to the franchise.

Freestanding brand A brand used for a single product, unconnected with other products in the manufacturer's range.

Functionality What a product does for the buyer and user; the utility it offers the user; what he or she can do with it. It is not the product itself but its functionality that creates a market for it.

Goods A product consisting predominantly of tangible values. Almost all goods, however, have intangible values to a greater or lesser extent.

Group discussion (1) A qualitative research technique in which a group of about eight people is invited to a neutral venue to discuss a given subject, for example hand-held power tools. The principle is the same as in a depth interview, except that group dynamics help to make the discussion livelier and more wide-ranging. (2) 'A marketing seance' (J. Murphy, *Brand Strategy*).

High technology (*high-tech*) A term with vague meaning. This covers electronics, data technology, telecommunications, medical technology and bio-chemistry. In order to be classed as a high-tech company, one definition is that at least 35 per cent of staff should have a technical qualification, and at least 15 per cent of sales should be used for R&D. Another definition states that the company must employ twice as many scientists and engineers and invest twice as much in R&D as the average of all manufacturing companies in the country.

Intangibles 'Intangible' – incapable of being touched. (1) Intangible assets – trade marks, copyrights, patents, design rights, proprietary expertise, databases, etc. (2) Intangible brand attributes – brand names, logos, graphics, colours, shapes and smells. (3) Intangible brand values – useful qualities attributed to the brand through feelings and beliefs.

Joint venture (1) Two or more parties establish or control a joint venture company. This may be either a newly formed or a pre-existing company. (2) Two or more parties establish a partnership. (3) Contractual arrangement where two parties agree to share risk to promote activity in an area of common interest. This occurs without a corporate shell representing the legal personality of the joint venture. This is a contractual joint venture.

Launch The initial marketing of a new product in a particular market. The way in which the launch is carried out greatly affects the product's profitability throughout its life-cycle.

Licensing Where the business allows third parties to use certain of the business's technology or intellectual property under strict, regulated control.

Market leader A company that has achieved a commanding position – either in scale (e.g. British Airways) or influence (e.g. Virgin) – within its field. This leading position often comes about because the company was the first to market a certain type of product and, with the protection of a patent, has managed to consolidate its position before direct competition was possible. Alternatively, a company may overtake a previous market leader through greater efficiency and skilful positioning.

Market position A measure of the position of a company or product on a market. Defined as market share multiplied by share of mind.

Market segment A group of customers who (a) share the same needs and values, (b) can be expected to respond in much the same way to a company's offering, and (c) command enough purchasing power among to be of strategic importance to the company.

Market share A company's share of total sales of a given category of product on a given market.

Mass marketing Simultaneous standardized marketing to a very large target market through mass media. Other names for the same thing are market aggregation and undifferentiated marketing.

Masterbrand A brand name that dominates all products or services in a range or across a business. Sometimes used with sub-brands, sometimes used with alpha or numeric signifiers (see also Monolithic Brand). Audi, Durex, Nescafé and Lego, for example, are all used as masterbrands.

Monolithic brand A single brand name that is used to 'masterbrand' all products or services in a range. Individual products are nearly always identified by alpha or numeric signifiers. Companies like Mercedes and BMW favour such systems.

Multibrand strategy or **multiple branding** Marketing of two or more mutually competing products under different brand names by the same company. The motive may be that the company wishes to create internal competition to promote efficiency, or to differentiate its offering to different market segments, or to get maximum mileage out of established brands that it has acquired. When a company has achieved a dominant market share, multibrand strategy may be its only option for increasing sales still further without sacrificing profitability. For example, Lever Brothers sells washing powders under the Persil, Omo and Surf names, Cadbury sells chocolates under the Dairy Milk, Bournville and Fruit and Nut names, Heinz sells canned convenience foods under the Baked Beans, Spaghetti Hoops and Alphabetti Spaghetti names.

Names There are three basic categories of brand (or corporate) name:

1. *Descriptive name* – a name which describes the product or service for which it is intended e.g. TALKING PAGES.
2. *Associative name* – a name which alludes to an aspect or benefit of the product or service, often by means of an original or striking image or idea e.g. VISA.

3. *Freestanding name* – a name which has no link to the product or service but which might have meaning of its own e.g. PENGUIN.

The following are also helpful:

4. *Abstract name* – a name which is entirely invented and has no meaning of its own e.g. ZENECA. Abstract names are a sub-set of freestanding names because they also have no link to the product of service.

5. *Coined name* – any name which is in some way invented. Coined names can be descriptive (CO-CREATE), associative (IMATION) and freestanding/abstract (ZENECA).

Niche marketing Marketing adapted to the needs, wishes and expectations of small, precisely defined groups of individuals. A form of market segmentation, but aimed at very small segments. Niche marketing characteristically uses selective media.

OEM market OEM stands for Original Equipment Manufacturers. The OEM market consists of companies that use another company's product as a component in their own production. A manufacturer of ball bearings, for example, sells both to OEM customers who build the bearings into machines, and to end-users who need the bearings as spare parts for machines that they have bought from the OEMs. Most manufacturing companies thus have an OEM market and a replacement market. The latter is usually called the MRO market or aftermarket.

Offering What a company offers for sale to customers. An offering includes the product and its design, features, quality, packaging, distribution, etc., together with associated services such as financing, warranties and installation. The name and brand of the product are also part of the offering. Determining exactly what the company is offering to whom is one of the most crucial aspects of marketing. Like many other important aspects, it is often taken so much for granted that it is not done properly. Fuzzy offerings, or no offerings at all, are common causes of inefficiency in marketing communications.

Partnership The joining of two or more parties who fulfil the legal definition of a Partnership – 'the relation which subsists between two persons carrying out a business in common with a view to profit'.

Passing off The name given to a legal action brought to protect the 'reputation' of a particular trademark/brand/get-up. Essentially, passing off is like a cake in that it requires several ingredients to succeed. These ingredients are that the trademark/brand/get-up has acquired a reputation through use, that the mark/brand/get-up against which the complaint is made is a misrepresentation of the trademark/brand/get-up which is claiming the reputation, that this is resulting (or is likely to result) in confusion, and is also resulting (or is likely to result) in damage being caused to the goodwill/business of the proprietor of the trademark/brand/ get-up which is suing for passing off. As with a cake, if any of these ingredients are missing, the passing-off action will fail. In essence, the action is designed to prevent others from trading on the reputation/ goodwill of an existing trademark/brand/get-up. The action is only available in those countries which recognize unregistered trademark rights (for example the UK and USA). In some countries, it is called 'unfair competition action'.

Perceptual mapping Graphic analysis and presentation of where actual and potential customers place a product or supplier in relation to other products and suppliers. Most perceptual maps show only two dimensions at a time, for example price on the ordinate and quality on the abscissa. Two-dimensional maps are easy to understand, but show only part of the truth. It is seldom possible to squeeze the complex reality of a market into two dimensions. There also are methods of graphically analysing and presenting measurement data in three or more dimensions, but they are seldom used because they are difficult for anybody except research experts and statisticians to grasp!

Positioning statement A written description of (a) the position that a company wishes itself, its product or its brand to occupy in the minds of a defined target audience and (b) how the company plans to go about capturing and defending its chosen position.

Power branding A strategy in which every product in a company's range has its own brand name which functions independently, unsupported by either the company's corporate brand or its other product brands. Power branding is a resource-intensive strategy, since each brand must be commercially promoted and legally protected. This strategy is used mainly by manufacturers of consumer goods. Lever's and Procter & Gamble's detergents are good examples of power brands.

Procurement The strict rules of public procurement apply where an alliance involves the provision of goods or services to your brand. This effects the selection process by which you choose a third party. This must be achieved via a tendering process.

Relative market share Your own company's market share compared to those of your competitors. A large share confers advantages of scale in product development, manufacturing and marketing. It also puts you in a stronger position in the minds of customers, with the result that they tend to buy your product in preference to somebody else's, and that you can charge a higher price for it.

Relaunch Reintroducing a product on a specific market. The term implies that the company has previously marketed the product but stopped marketing it, maybe because it had technical defects or was not profitable enough. A relaunched product has usually undergone one or more changes. It may, for example, be technically modified, rebranded, distributed through different channels or repositioned.

Repositioning Communications activities to give an existing product a new position in customers' minds and so expanding or otherwise altering its potential market. Many potentially valuable products lead an obscure existence because they were launched or positioned in an inadequate manner. It is almost always possible to enhance the value of such products by repositioning them.

Rollout A process in which a company concentrates its efforts on its geographical markets one at a time to avoid spreading its resources too thinly. Another advantage is that marketing can be made successively more efficient thanks to feedback of experience.

Selective media Media that, unlike mass media, reach only small and identifiable groups of people, for example members of a particular profession or industry or other groups defined by geographic, demographic or psychographic data.

Service A product consisting predominantly of intangible values. 'A service is something that you can buy and sell, but not drop on your foot' (*The Economist*). In this sense, a service is something that you do for somebody.

Share of mind The number of potential customers for your product who regard your company or brand as the best choice. Market share measures the width of a company's market position. Share of mind measures its depth.

Sponsorship Finance is provided in exchange for brand visibility within the activity sponsored.

Tangibles 'Tangible' – capable of being touched. (1) Tangible assets – manufacturing plant, bricks and mortar, cash, investments, etc. (2) Tangible brand attributes – the product and its packaging. (3) Tangible brand values – useful qualities of the brand known to exist through experience and knowledge.

Target market The market segment or group of customers that a company has decided to serve, and at which it consequently aims its marketing activities.

Top-of-mind What is present in the uppermost level of consciousness; the manufacturer or brand that people in market surveys name first when asked to list products in a specific category. Top-of-mind is the highest degree of share of mind. To attain that position, a company normally needs to have the largest share of communications ('voice') in its category.

Trademark 'Any sign capable of being represented graphically which is capable of distinguishing goods or services of one undertaking from those of another undertaking' (UK Trade Marks Act 1994).

Trademark infringement A trademark registration is infringed by the unauthorized use of the registered trade mark, or of one which is confusingly similar to it, on the registered goods or services, or in certain circumstances on similar or dissimilar goods and services.

User segmentation Division of potential customers into market segments according to how and for what purpose they use a product. Do they use it for cleaning their teeth or for making cakes (baking powder)? For oiling their hair or for frying food? (True story concerning use of Brylcreem in Nigeria). As a decongestant chest rub or as an aphrodisiac? (True story concerning Ribby Rub in Caribbean).

Index